This book is dedicated to three men. Each has molded my personality, emotions, and intellect in his own unique, loving manner. And each has played a major role in helping this book become a reality. I love these men with all my heart.

First and foremost is the Lord Jesus Christ, to whom I owe my spiritual life and from whom comes my inspiration and direction in everything.

Second is my natural father, John Greenman, to whom I owe my physical life and from whom came my life's watchword when he once told me I could do anything. This book is part of his prophecy fulfilled.

Third is my pastor and dearest friend, Dale Brooks, to whom I owe every facet of my ministry and much of my maturity. This book is part of his love multiplied.

I present *How To Find Your Purpose In Life* with joy, love, and insufficient thanks in honor of these men.

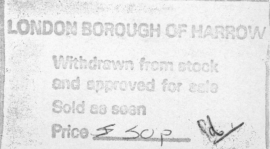

ACKNOWLEDGEMENTS

Every worthwhile endeavor followed through to completion is the product of many interested minds, hearts, and hands. The production of this book has enjoyed the talents and energies of many such interested folks. Two stand high above the rest.

First and most important is my wife, Meg. Even though she never typed a line, collated a chapter, or proofread a single word, she furnished me with the one ingredient every author so desperately needs—encouragement. Her consistent flow of positive words about this work became my strength, pulling me through many days and nights of doubt and mental fatigue. I love you, Meg.

Second and never least is Barbara Thomas. Thousands of pages, hundreds of corrections, and weeks of bleery-eyed nights before her word-processor made for a professional quality I could never have achieved alone. Her enthusiasm was as tireless as her fingers on the typewriter keyboard. My thanks and love to you, Barbara, come straight from the heart.

CONTENTS

PREFACE

For several years I have been aware of a great need within the Body of Christ. That need has been echoed again and again by the hundreds of brethren I have counseled across this country and in my home church. The need is to find the reason they are alive on planet Earth. "What's my purpose for being here?" "What am I supposed to do with my life?" "Who am I?" Having asked these very questions myself, I found it easy to sympathize. Fortunately, I have also been able to offer some solid, proven answers to those often desperate counselees.

Like me, those people were honest and sincere in beseeching the Lord on this matter. They longed to know the purpose for their lives and perform the bidding of their King. My own desire led me to the discovery of the principles that revealed God's plan for my life. These principles are so practical that they can be applied to anyone's personal endeavors, be it a major goal in life or a short-range matter. I have had the pleasure of sharing these same principles with hundreds of such seekers for several years with great results. (See "SonDance: A Testimony" at the end of this book.) Having only touched the tip of the counseling iceberg on this subject, I felt that a book was the only way to reach the thousands and perhaps millions of believers still seeking their life's vision.

But this need in the individual believer has created a need within the church at large. Due to the fact that a great number of Christians have, as yet, not found their personal plans, the overall plan of the church has thus been stifled. When members of a body have no idea of their specific place and function, the entire body is affected. Aimless hands and feet cannot direct the abilities of a body out of control. Only by dealing with the individual members can we hope to strengthen the power of the entire church. This book is an attempt to assist the Body of Christ in that effort.

But the need does not stop at the church. The world is the real treasure that we seek to place at the feet of our Lord. There are literally billions of godless people waiting for the Church of the Lord Jesus Christ to rise up in all of its power and glory to rescue them. The Church is the only hope these starving multitudes have.

But the Church is individuals. It is the individual believer who will save the lives of millions with the gospel of Jesus Christ. If those believers do not find their God-ordained place and live in it, the effectiveness of the Church to meet the world's need for life will be impossible. We must enlighten the individual, thereby enlightening the Church, which will enlighten the darkening world.

A Final Note

When I began to search for my own purpose, I had no publication such as this to turn to and no counselor to advise me. I felt terribly alone. I did possess one element, however, that proved to be all I needed to get the ball rolling in the right direction: I had an unshakable faith in God—pure, childlike faith that says, "My Dad can do anything, and He will take care of me." This faith allowed me to believe, without reservation, whatever I read in the Scriptures. Constantly attempting to put into practice that which I read or heard taught from the Bible, I just knew that the Lord would not let me down.

I remember reading John 10:27, which says that as the Lord's sheep I would know His voice and follow Him. Knowing that word had to be true, I soon found myself praying, "Father, I'm not sure what Your voice sounds like; but I know that if You said I would hear it, then I will. I want to follow You. So this is what I am going to do: When I pray and ask You things, You had better be the first one to speak because that is the voice I will follow."

That was not the prayer of pride or arrogance but one of simple faith. The Lord honored my prayer. Soon He and I were conversing like old friends, and it has only gotten better over the years. During our times of communion, God has shared with me the detailed workings of His plan for my life. This close relationship did not come overnight. It has taken years to receive such direction, and I am still receiving more instructions all the time.

I have learned the meaning of "a still small voice" and also the "thunder and lightning" of God's authority. He has become my best friend, teacher, counselor, and disciplinarian. He applauds my victories and comforts my defeats. He consoles my mistakes and punishes my disobedience. I have felt the might of the Lord's healing power flow through me and the gentleness of His compassion caress through my words. I have experienced God's supernatural power and His insight into my humanness.

I have a real relationship with the Almighty who created me. He is truly my Father and just as truly my God. He is my most valued possession. Do I know *all* about Him? Of course not. But I am content with the fact that He knows all about me and still chooses to love and use me to His glory.

Of all I can teach anyone in this book, or others like it, this one truth is essential: *A meaningful and intimate relationship with the Lord must be the ultimate goal of every life; for only when we have acquired such a relationship can we hope to find and live out the purpose He has for our lives.* That is my prayer for you. God bless you!

Bill Greenman

1
GOD HAS A PLAN FOR YOU

In his letter to the Colossians, the apostle Paul mentioned the prayer he prayed continually for that body of believers. (See Colossians 1:9-11.) When I began my commitment to the Lordship of Christ, I took that prayer for my own. Daily I would read it and claim its truth for my life. As God's child, I wanted the perfect will of the Father to be at work in me and desired to be filled with His wisdom and plan for me.

I recited that set of scriptures thousands of times, and before long the revelation of its words became fact. Through my daily walk with the Lord, I came to know and formulate the information in the following pages. This information was the road to finding my purpose in life. It has changed me from a seemingly directionless disciple into a useful and on-target member of the Body of the Lord.

These same principles will work for you. Why? Because they are from God's Word and have been proved over and over again in my own life and the lives of others who applied them. These are not hyper-spiritual or spooky ritual, just simple Bible truths.

The apostle Paul admonishes his beloved pupil, Timothy, to fulfill the ministry God has given him in 2 Timothy 4:5-7. Paul follows this instruction by stating that he himself has fulfilled his own God-given ministry: "I have fought a good fight, I have finished my course, I have kept the faith."

If you are anything like me, and I am pretty sure you are, then these words from Paul invoke a sense of envy. When it is our time to leave this life, all of us would like to say we have run the race the Lord has set before us and that we did not faint in our faith along the way. Unfortunately, most of us are more apt to cry that we fought the fight, but our eyes were so swollen from the beating that we couldn't find the course, let alone keep the faith! If, like me, that seems to be your song, let me assure you that the Lord has a new tune for you.

God has a specific and special course for your life. It is a course filled with fun, adversity, joy, hard work, and victory. It is the most exciting and fulfilling course you could ever hope to run. What is your course? Frankly, I haven't the faintest idea. But by the time you are finished with this book, you will be well on your way to discovering that course for yourself. You will also have acquired the knowledge to make it happen.

Why A Vision?

Before we begin to discover *how* to find your personal purpose in life, let's take time to establish the truth of *why* you need a purpose.

When I was an assistant pastor, the questions most frequently asked of me in counseling sessions were: "Why am I here?"; "What is my purpose in life?"; and, "What is it that God wants me to do?" Those sincere questions usually flowed from hearts in great turmoil because they did not know the answers. God states in the following verses that such turmoil comes to those who do not know their purpose in life or do not have a vision: "Where there is no vision the people perish" (Proverbs 29:18, *KJV*). "My people are destroyed for lack of knowledge" (Hosea 4:6).

Let's look specifically at Proverbs 29:18. The *New American Standard Bible* states, "Where there is no vision the people are unrestrained." The word "vision," according to the margin of this translation, means *revelation*. This word can also be translated as "mental sight" or "a revealed word from God." The word "unrestrained" denotes the absence of guidance or direction.

A restraint, as referred to in this verse, is like a bit in a horse's mouth. The restraint is not used to bind the horse but to direct him. In other words, if you do not have a mental image—a revelation of God's purpose for you—you will be without

17

direction, having no means of His guidance in your life. You will be perishing! On the other hand, if you do have a revealed word from God, you *will* be restrained. You will be guided. You will have purpose and direction. *You will have life!*

God does not want us to perish. He does not want us to be destroyed just because we lack knowledge of His plan for our lives. In 1 Corinthians chapter twelve, the Lord states that not only does He have an assigned spot for each one of His children but that He will personally place us in it: "But now God has placed the members, each one of them, in the body, just as He desired" (1 Corinthians 12:18).

If you have not yet discovered your God-ordained place in life, you will not have the ability to be fully directed by Him. You may have visions, dreams, and goals you want to attain, and they may motivate you. They may even give you purpose and direction for a time. But only God's purpose, for you as an individual, will bring you the abundant, meaningful life both you and He desire you to experience.

Let me use myself as an example. In the naivete of my early Christian life, I thought "fire insurance" was all there was to salvation. I continued to make plans according to *my* desires, *my* dreams, and the direction *I* wanted to take. I eventually became a full-time circus performer, thinking that fulfilling the dream of being a professional entertainer, which had been in my heart since I was a child, was success. After five long years as a Christian, with *me* in control of my life instead of Christ, I found out differently.

I discovered that no matter how much we may proclaim the reality of Jesus as our *Savior,* our lives are empty without Jesus as our *Lord.* And I discovered the truth of Proverbs 29:18. Because I did not have a revealed word from God, I did not have *God's* guidance active in my life. Instead, I had my own and was, therefore, perishing. There was a void in my life. Finally realizing my failure, I cried out to God, "Okay! Father, no longer my will but Your will be done in my life!" It was then that both my spiritual and natural life ignited.

Almost immediately, God planted His vision of a Christ-centered circus in my heart. That vision gave me new purpose and fulfilled me in a way no other dream had done. I am now totally directed by that vision and purpose. I have been restrained, directed, and guided because of it. My total motivation stems from the vision because it is God's purpose and plan for my life.

God has a vision—a purpose and plan—for your life. He desires to share it with you. That purpose and vision will restrain, lead, and guide you for the rest of your life. It will save you from destruction. That vision is not some spooky, hyperspiritual quest. It is God's perfect will for you personally. I guarantee you, there is no greater feeling of security in the entire world than living out His perfect will for your life.

Ultimate success is placing all that you are into God's hands to do with as He pleases. The day I made that decision was the day my life took off like a rocket. I believe yours will, too. Find your vision. Find direction. Find your purpose in life!

2
YOUR PLACE IN THE SON

You have a specific place in God's master plan, a place only *you* can fulfill—a place you will occupy to fulfill the destiny He ordained for you. It will satisfy the deepest longing of your being. But, in this chapter, I also wish to deal with the general vision the Lord has for you and every Christian.

The Father has set certain things (from which none of us is exempt) before His Church to accomplish. These universal orders will not only cause the master plan of God to be realized by His Body but will also assist in the preparation of the individual believer to live out his or her vision.

In Matthew 5:14-16, the Lord Jesus makes a bold and far-reaching proclamation to His followers:

> "You are the light of the world. A city set on a hill cannot be hidden. Nor do men light a lamp, and put it under the peck-measure, but on the lampstand;

and it gives light to all who are in the house. Let your light shine before men in such a way that they may see your good works, and glorify your Father who is in heaven."

What a mandate! What a powerful commission! By making this statement, Jesus is equating His Church with Himself in its ability to bring God into a world that does not know Him. He is clearly saying, "*You* be the light now. I've been the light. Go do what I did. Be a giver. Be a healer. Be a vessel for the power of God to flow through to meet the needs of people. *Let* your good deeds reflect the glory of God. Don't be afraid, and don't hide what I am giving you. Men in a dark place are drawn to the light. Be that light for them." What a thrilling privilege we are given in these verses!

As exciting as Christ's command is, much lies behind its seemingly simple message. For us to be the light of the world requires more than a directive from Jesus' lips. If we fail to put wings to His words, they will never find reality in our lives. Notice that this small but pivotal set of letters spell the word "let." With that one word, Jesus unquestionably places responsibility for the attaining of His words on the all-too-human shoulders of His Church. The choice is unequivocally *ours*.

There was a time when the church chose to rebel against this order. That decision plunged this world into the most vile time of its existence, which we appropriately call the Dark Ages. During this time, the Word of God was almost lost. The candle of God's church flickered as if to go out. But the Lord always had a people to bear His light, and they slowly emerged again to spread the good news of His love.

Perhaps you are in a dark age or have not yet discovered how to "let" your light shine. If so, here are some simple steps you can take. They comprise the items of the universal vision God has for His children and are general marching orders to be followed by all.

Maintain Lordship

Maintaining Lordship is the first of three sections of this general vision God has for His people. (See Figure 2-A.) In Matthew 6:33 we find the famous passage, "Seek ye first the kingdom of God, and His righteousness; and all these things shall be added unto you" (*KJV*).

First of all, we must understand what is meant by the word "seek." In this verse, the Greek word we translate as "seek" is taken from the Hebrew word for *worship*. In fact, upon studying both Old and New Testaments, I discovered only five different words that translated into the English word seek. In all but one of those translations either the first or secondary meaning is defined as worship or prayer, and all have a root meaning of searching for something.

To seek, then, means to search for through prayer and worship. We need not dig into mounds of theological volumes or climb pinnacled mountains to holy temples in search of the Lord or His Kingdom. We need only to lift our voices and bend our knees daily in worship and prayerful communion to seek Him and His Kingdom.

The Bible is quite clear on this subject:

> Then Jesus said to him, "Begone, Satan! For it is written, 'You shall worship the Lord your God, and serve Him only' "—Matthew 4:10.

> I urge you therefore, brethren, by the mercies of God, to present your bodies a living and holy sacrifice, acceptable to God, which is your spiritual service of worship. And do not be conformed to the world, but be transformed by the renewing of your mind, that you may prove what the will of God is, that which is good and acceptable and perfect—Romans 12:1-2.

> The twenty-four elders will fall down before Him who sits on the throne, and will worship Him who lives forever and ever, and will cast their crowns before the throne—Revelation 4:10.

Worship of the Lord is the first order of maintaining Lordship. These verses state the Lord's view of such worship. Not only are we to worship the Lord God and Him only, but He clearly states that Jesus is the receiver of our praises. Even our physical bodies are to be a form of worship. Our Father leaves no room for speculation. He orders us to worship and then explains to whom our worship is extended. Finally, He informs us how our worship is to be given. *Our very lives* are to become a worship unto the Lord.

The second item under maintaining Lordship is the *study of God's Word*. In Matthew 4:4, Jesus states the importance of the Word of God: "But He answered and said, 'It is written, "Man shall not live on bread alone, but on every word that proceeds out of the mouth of God." ' "

God's Word is actually more important than food for our bodies. Not that we should neglect the replenishing of our physical form with proper foods, but we must realize that the Word of God is even more needed by our spirits. Why? Second Timothy 3:16-17 gives us the answer. Food stuffs can only energize the body, but the Word can touch our entire being: "All Scripture is inspired by God and profitable for teaching, for reproof, for correction, for training in righteousness; that the man of God may be adequate, equipped for every good work."

The Word of God is a multi-faceted instrument with which the Father can mold and shape us into the people we were meant to be. It can correct a fault, instruct in service, convict, or reprove. God's life-changing Word has the supernatural ability to turn a total rebel into a totally godly man. But, as with anything in God's Kingdom, *we* have the final say in how much, if at all, His Word will affect us. We must make a daily effort to study and understand the scriptures.

The Holy Spirit is our teacher in this effort, for He will take what we are studying and reveal its full meaning to us. This knowledge is known as *revelation* and was announced by Christ as the rock upon which He would construct His Church: "Flesh and blood did not reveal this to you, but My Father who is in heaven. And I also say to you that you are Peter, and upon this rock I will build My church; and the gates of Hades shall not overpower it" (Matthew 16:17-18). The Holy Spirit, however, can only reveal that word which we put inside us. We must visit the equipment shed before the equipper can shell out the necessary item.

The final needed point to maintaining the Lordship of Christ in our lives is that of *obedience*. Jesus did not mince words on the subject: "And why do you call Me, 'Lord, Lord,' and do not do what I say?" (Luke 6:46). "But prove yourselves doers of the word, and not merely hearers who delude themselves" (James 1:22).

Doing whatever the Holy Spirit reveals to you from the Word of God is mandatory. (We will discuss in later chapters how to hear and confirm

God's voice in your personal prayer time.) Many people *claim* to be believers, but it is the *doer* who will stand when the flood waters of life subside. The point is that the storms will come against us regardless of how prepared we are. Digging deep into the solid rock of God's Word through the doing of that Word brings a guarantee of successful preparation.

Local Living

Functioning in a local church body comprises the second section of our general commission. In 1 Corinthians chapter twelve, we have a vivid description of how the Lord sees His Church. He likens it to the human body, which has many members that make up the whole. In verse twelve, Paul asserts that we are all members of one Body, denoting the universal Body of believers past, present, and future. But the passage also mentions the local aspect of church membership in verse eighteen. Here the writer states that God will personally place each of us in the specific section of the Body where we belong. Such precise placement can only be realized at a local church level. This spot we are singularly molded for allows us and the body we enter to operate at full capacity.

To help us further understand His view on this matter, God indicates that, as in the human body, there should be no divisiveness between members.

No one believer is more important than any other, and no member should either exalt himself or degrade others.

Clearly spoken, we need one another:

> If the foot should say, "Because I am not a hand, I am not a part of the body," it is not for this reason any the less a part of the body. And if the ear should say, "Because I am not an eye, I am not a part of the body," it is not for this reason any the less a part of the body. If the whole body were an eye, where would the hearing be? If the whole were hearing, where would the sense of smell be? . . . And if they were all one member, where would the body be? But now there are many members, but one body. And the eye cannot say to the hand, "I have no need of you"; or again the head to the feet, "I have no need of you. . . . There should be no division in the body, but that the members should have the same care for one another. And if one member suffers, all the members suffer with it; if one member is honored, all the members rejoice with it. Now you are Christ's body, and individually members of it—1 Corinthians 12:15-17, 19-21, 25-27.

This scriptural analogy is both informative and reassuring. But our God does not leave us without explicit instruction. Within the pages of the New Testament are found thirty specific orders directing believers on how to live as loving members of Christ's Church. These orders are only possible to follow at the local level, in which relationships have been established. Such meaningful relationships will require time and effort to build. A commitment to a local body of Christ is the only answer to their fulfillment. Again, obedience or rebellion are the only choices a believer has.

The following is what I call the check list of church success. If we can fulfill this list, we are well on the way to living the life Christ meant each of us to experience.

Love one another (John 13:34,35)
Members of one another (Romans 12:5)
Devoted to one another (Romans 12:10a)
Outdo one another in showing honor (Romans 12:10b)
Rejoice with one another (Romans 12:15a)
Weep with one another (Romans 12:15b)
Same mind toward one another (Romans 12:16)
Not judge one another (Romans 14:13)
Accept one another (Romans 15:7)
Build up one another (Romans 15:14)
Greet one another (Romans 16:16)
Wait for one another (1 Corinthians 11:33)
Care for one another (1 Corinthians 12:25)

Serve one another (Galatians 5:13)
Bear one another's burdens (Galatians 6:2)
Be kind to one another (Ephesians 4:32a)
Forgive one another (Ephesians 4:32b)
Submit to one another (Ephesians 5:21)
Counsel one another (Colossians 3:13)
Bearing with one another (1 Thessolonians 5:11a)
Encourage one another (1 Thessolonians 11b)
Stir up one another (Hebrews 10:24)
Don't speak evil against one another (James 4:11)
Don't grumble against one another (James 5:9)
Confess faults to one another (James 5:16a)
Pray for one another (James 5:16b)
Be hospitable to one another (1 Peter 4:9)
Minister gifts to one another (1 Peter 4:10)
Clothed with humility to one another (1 Peter 5:5)
Fellowship with one another (1 John 12:5)

Exposing the Light

The third and final section of the general commission to believers is that of sharing our new life with others who have never met Jesus. This is a major aspect of letting your light shine. It is known as *being a witness.* Jesus' final words, before His ascension, echoed this call:

And He said to them, "Go into all the world and preach the gospel to all creation. He who has believed and has been baptized shall be saved; but he who has disbelieved shall be condemned. And these signs will follow those who have believed: in My name they will cast out demons, they will speak with new tongues; they will pick up serpents, and if they drink any deadly poison, it shall not hurt them; they will lay hands on the sick and they will recover''—Mark 16:15-18.

"All authority has been given to Me in heaven and on earth. Go therefore and make disciples of all nations, baptizing them in the name of the Father and the Son and the Holy Spirit, teaching them to observe all that I commanded you; and lo, I am with you always, even to the end of the age''— Matthew 28:18-20.

"But you shall receive power when the Holy Spirit has come upon you; and you shall be My witnesses both in Jerusalem, and in all Judea and Samaria, and even to the remotest part of the earth''— Acts 1:8.

These passages explain the full intent of our Father in the area of witnessing for His Son, Jesus.

We are to preach, teach, administer God's healing power, deliver the captives of Satan, and baptize those who believe. This is no passive witness but a very aggressive one—aggressive in the sense that we are to reach out boldly to people who are on their way to a God-less hell. We are not to wax fat and happy on our new-found glory in Christ. We are to give it away.

Billions of people are just like we were and need what we have. Sharing our faith in Christ is our privilege and, actually, the only real reason we are left on this planet after receiving Jesus as Lord. Christ relinquished the task of informing people about Himself to His Church and gave clear instructions on how it should be done. It is up to us and us alone. Angels cannot preach. The dead cannot teach. Only the living Church of Jesus Christ can be His witness:

> For "Whoever will call upon the name of the Lord will be saved." How then shall they call upon Him in whom they have not believed? And how shall they believe in Him whom they have not heard? And how shall they hear without a preacher? And how shall they preach unless they are sent? Just as it is written, "How beautiful are the feet of those who bring glad tidings of good things!" However, they did not all heed the glad tidings; for Isaiah says, "Lord, who has

believed our report?'' So faith comes
from hearing and hearing by the word
of Christ—Romans 10:13-17.

Countless books have been written about witnessing. Courses in personal evangelism abound.
But if you want a clear, simple definition of being
a successful witness for Christ, remember this
phrase: *Find a need and meet it*. With the power
of God at your disposal, that statement transcends
the impossible. "And Jesus said to him, 'If you can!
All things are possible to him who believes' "
(Mark 9:23). Do all in your ability to educate yourself on sharing the gospel and making disciples.
It is the most exciting and rewarding element of
the Christian life.

Letting your light shine before men is your
fundamental purpose as part of the universal Body
of Christ. Each of us is to take that truth and apply
it daily to an ever darkening world. Through the
constant monitoring of our lives, we can fulfill the
commission left by Jesus and actually proclaim the
good news into every country on earth. This
requires each of us buckling down to the task of
maintaining the Lordship of Christ in our lives
through daily worship, Word study, and obedience.

We need to discover our place in a local body
of believers and live out our personal visions while
assisting with the body's vision. Opening
ourselves to the joys and heartaches of giving is
mandatory. Our lives must become an example of

living to give. And, of course, the very reason for the shining of our brilliant light is to witness about the glories of our God and King. Boldly, yet meekly, displaying Christ to a hurting world through us is God's anointed and unfathomable plan. It will take each of us, to the man, to pull it off.

I find it amazing that such an all-powerful God can trust such a monumental and exacting task to such a fragile and vulnerable creature as man. But that is the miracle of God, for He actually lives His life through us. Yes, the general vision for Christ's Church is a mighty one. Your personal purpose in life will fit right into it. In fact, the Lord will even endow you with special gifts to assist you to that end.

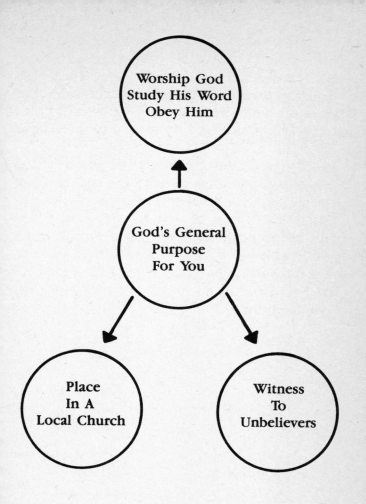

Figure 2-A

35

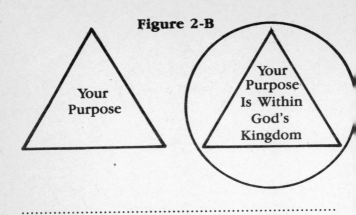

Figure 2-B

Your Purpose

Your Purpose Is Within God's Kingdom

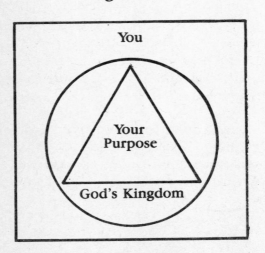

Figure 2-C

You

Your Purpose

God's Kingdom

Your Purpose Is Within God's Kingdom.
God's Kingdom Is Within You.
Therefore, Your Purpose Is Within You.

3

YOU ARE GIFTED

The Lord in His infinite wisdom has chosen to endow every one of His children with certain gifts. Each gift has a specific function and place in the overall picture of His will for this age. These gifts are given to assist the individual believer in his or her attempt to live out God's purpose for his or her life. The primary objective for these gifts is identified in God's Word as that of ministering to His Body:

As each one has received a special gift, employ it in serving one another, as good stewards of the manifold grace of God—Philippians 4:10.

For just as we have many members in one body and all the members do not have the same function, so we, who are many, are one body in Christ, and individually members one of another.

And since we have gifts that differ
according to the grace given to us—
Romans 12:4-6.

According to these verses, the main purpose
individual members of the church are given gifts
is to serve one another. Our personal vision will
be enhanced by the gifts entrusted to us by our
heavenly Father. By effectively operating in these
gifts as singular believers, we will enhance the
overall effectiveness of Christ's Body. The sharing of our gifts with one another will complete
the Body we are part of. My gifts will complement
yours, and yours will complement mine.

Although I am definitely not gifted in math, my
wife takes over with ease. Where she may lack
understanding of the difference between motor oil
and transmission fluid, I take over (quickly!).

The Body of Christ is to function in a similar
manner, with every joint supplying the gift needed
for the moment. "From whom the whole body,
being fitted and held together by that which every
joint supplies, according to the proper working
of each individual part, causes the growth of the
body for the building up of itself in love"
(Ephesians 4:16).

Whether it be our natural gifts or our spiritual
ones, all are meant to enhance and complete the
Body of Christ. No gift is given to a believer solely
for self-gratification. We are to share our gifts as
freely as we have received them: "Heal the sick,

raise the dead, cleanse the lepers, cast out demons; freely you have received, freely give'' (Matthew 10:8).

The Natural Gifts

Although this chapter will deal primarily with the subject of spiritual gifts, I will take a moment to discuss the field of natural gifts our Maker blesses us with. This category of gifts includes both the physical and the intellectual attributes of a human being. Let's take a look at the physical first.

Physical gifts include talents that display expertise or above normal control of one's body. Such things as running, jumping, throwing, and swimming would be good examples. A gifted person would find activities simple to learn and easy to perfect. You know the guy. The first time he picks up a baseball he's striking out major leaguers. Or the girl who buys a tennis racket one day, and by next week she's on T.V. playing Wimbledon. Are these gross exaggerations? To be sure. But to someone who throws a frisbee like a shot put, it seems all too close to reality. The gifted athlete stands out.

Not all natural gifts in the physical category come under the heading of sports or athletics, however. Such gifts as singing, playing a musical instrument, drawing, sculpting, acting, and even mime also fit under this heading. These gifts are easily recognized. Many can sing, but few have a three or four octave range. A multitude may "tickle the ivories" of a piano, but few pack Carnegie Hall for a concert. Again, a gifted person will be noticed easily among the average.

Now let's take a peek at the intellectual gifts. Intellectual gifts primarily deal with the abilities of mental power. By that I do not allude to the forms of mind over matter that seem to bend spoons and move small objects. That is purely demonic in origin and not worth explaining here. Mental power, as I will refer to it, is the above normal ability to understand and apply what we learn in the mental realm.

We all know someone who excels beyond reason in mathematics or physics. Perhaps you personally have the capacity to remember the minutest detail of a book you've read or some event you witnessed. Another person may understand the workings of electricity to the point that he thoroughly confuses everyone while explaining it. Quite simply, we are talking about people who exemplify the word "genius" in one category of learning or another. They just have the "knack" for it. They are gifted.

I, myself, have never had a problem with memorizing anything. Most of my academic career was spent on the recreation fields instead of the study room because I could read something once and, with a couple of minutes review, remember the overall gist. Although this was a valuable asset at exam time, it made my school years a bit boring. It's not much fun throwing a football to yourself while everyone else is pouring over test materials.

But even with this enviable gift, I never became adept at some subjects. I was always totally frustrated by any math problem dealing with more than a plus, minus, or division sign. Memorizing for exams was never a problem, but apply it in the checkout line, no way! (As I mentioned, having a wife who is good in math definitely has its advantages.)

Let's face it. Some have it, and some don't! But as we face that truth, let's also consider Romans 2:11, which states that God is no respecter of persons. Simply put, this means that God does not covet my prayers above yours or your crystal shattering voice above mine. The gifts He entrusts to us are not due to an unequal love but instead to His wisdom in knowing what we will be able to handle accurately. Our Father knows exactly what course our lives will take, and He will only hold us accountable for the gifts He gives.

God is not a snaggle-toothed ogre waiting to strike His wards who step out of line and operate in an area they are not gifted in. Neither does He gleefully watch the despair of a well meaning disciple attempting to sing a solo on Sunday morning with a voice only meant for the shower on Saturday night. He is a loving Father who cares deeply for His children.

God bestows His gifts not only for the effective working of His will but also for our pleasure. I believe God enjoys a good swing on a trapeze or stroll on a slackwire as much as I do. What father has ever given a gift to one of his children without being filled with joy at the excitement that child experiences while using that gift to his or her own pleasure. Although the Lord does not give us our gifts solely for that reason, He does take delight in our pleasure.

So, if you happen to be a singer, musician, carpenter, mechanic, artist, designer, tight end, out fielder, or certified public accountant, your natural gifts are to be a blessing to your local body of Christ. If they aren't, you are both robbing other believers of your God-given talent and missing out on receiving the completion of your own life. At the end of this chapter, we will take a close look at the consequences of the use and abuse of our gifts.

Supernatural Abundance

A final thought on natural gifts: A person's natural gifts often are enlarged with his or her spiritual rebirth in Christ. For example, before I became a Christian I was interested in sports. I tried out for the football team, basketball team, and track team in high school. I proved to be sometimes average but more often mediocre. Organized sports and I jelled like water and oil. All I received for my pathetic high school career was two points in basketball, two winning games out of thirty-six games in football, a few second and third place track ribbons, a brain concussion, a cracked shin, a broken finger, and a dislocated knee! I was *not* gifted in organized sports.

But in 1971 a phenomenal thing began to occur. Shortly after giving my life to the Lord in the fall of that year, I took up karate. I excelled and actually became one of the best in my class. Two years later, I joined the Florida State University Flying High Circus. Within a few short weeks I was publicly performing several acts, including trapeze and the very difficult slackwire. My fellow circus performers were astounded by my ease in acquiring such skills and rapid development of my chosen acts. Before I left that university three years later, I had become a top performer, mastering almost every skill in the show from flying trapeze to juggling.

What made the difference between the mediocrity of my high school years and meteoric rise of my abilities in college? My only answer and my firm belief is that the Holy Spirit took my natural abilities and added supernatural abundance to them. Rest assured His motives were not for my self-pleasure only but for the edification of the Church and ministry to unbelievers. Although it took me several years to realize this, eventually I aligned my motives to match His. This humbling gave birth and substance to God's vision for me of directing a circus that would proclaim Jesus Christ as Lord. Your natural abilities, gifted and not, will find new power when Christ gains full control of your life.

The Spiritual Gifts

Spiritual gifts are those which are bestowed upon believers to assist them in the overall function of the entire Body of Christ. Does that sound like an echo of our discussion of natural gifts? Well, there is one major difference—the Holy Spirit. While natural gifts are affected by genetics, spiritual gifts are specifically distributed by the Holy Spirit and are not bound by a person's physical background. The only prerequisite for spiritual gifts is that the person be born again by the resurrection power of Jesus Christ. Natural gifts are found in everyone, regardless of their theological beliefs. But until the Holy Spirit has been given opportunity to dwell within a person, He cannot dispense the spiritual gifts.

The spiritual gifts that the Lord transmits to us actually have the power to transcend the laws and understanding of the natural world around us. They are given to allow the believer to perform specific acts and live out otherwise impossible assignments dictated by their position in Christ's Body. These gifts are listed in several books of the New Testament. Not everyone will experience every gift, and some believers may possess more than others, just as with the natural gifts. The point, however, is not how many one is given but what we do with the gifts we have received.

In 1 Corinthians 12:1, the apostle Paul expresses his concern that believers not be ignorant of God's spiritual gifts entrusted to them. That includes you and me. The Lord, through Paul, goes on to illuminate several of the gifts to which He refers.

Two different categories of gifts are mentioned in 1 Corinthians chapter twelve. Gifts in the first category are known as the gifts of the Holy Spirit. This tag is given because verse eleven mentions that it is the Holy Spirit who decides through whom and when these gifts will be activated. Also, these particular gifts are purely supernatural, being activated solely by the power of the Holy Spirit through an individual. They are usually given at a specific moment to meet a particular need. They are in contrast to the *motivating* and *ministerial* gifts, which operate in an ongoing fashion rather than at the timed discretion of the Lord. We will discuss these gifts later in the chapter.

The gifts of the Holy Spirit listed below, as well as those under the two headings just mentioned, will be given only a small explanation here. My intention is not to expound greatly upon these gifts but to share the basics of their workings so you may take this information and seek further insight on your own. These brief summaries will, however, offer valuable insight into the spiritual gifts the Lord has blessed *you* with. All of the spiritual gifts listed are, as I have mentioned, for sharing with others and not for self-gratification only.

The Gifts Of The Holy Spirit
(1 Corinthians 12:8-10)

These nine gifts are given by the Holy Spirit to whom He wills and when He wills. The key to operating in these gifts is to know how they are received. Being handed a gift is one thing, but knowing it has been given to you is another.

Although some people may experience certain physical feelings when the Holy Spirit is bestowing one of the following gifts upon you, such feelings are neither common nor necessary for the operation of these gifts. The only way a believer can have a clear understanding that the Holy Spirit is moving upon them in the area of one of these gifts is to establish the two-way communication necessary for such reception. This communication is only established through daily time spent with God. (We will also cover the language of the Holy Spirit in a later chapter. For, unless you understand His language, understanding and flowing with the Holy Spirit in the area of these gifts will be impossible.)

1. *Word Of Wisdom*

Wisdom is the ability to use what we know to the fullest extent. This gift takes the knowledge at hand and couples it with the supernatural overall understanding for meeting the particular need of the situation or individual. It is not dependent on our human areas of experience or knowledge.

2. *Word Of Knowledge*

Specific information, which one has no natural way of knowing, is revealed to the believer to meet a very specific need in the Body of Christ or an individual's life. Often this gift is found working with the gifts of miracles and healing.

Once while praying for the sick after one of our circus performances, the words "cystic fibrosis" came to my mind. I called for anyone with this disease to come forward, and only one young boy ventured forth from the audience of several hundred. When I rebuked the disease, the Lord instantly healed the young man. That was the word of knowledge given to allow the gift of healing to be administered.

3. *Faith*

The gift of faith is the supernatural ability to believe beyond all doubt that the Lord will do as He said He would. This ability will allow the recipient to stand unflinchingly in the face of what, in the natural realm, seem to be unbeatable odds. It can be both long and short range in its functioning.

One morning I was awakened by my wife to see a tornado heading straight for our house. While still in the daze of sleep, I pointed my finger at the roaring giant and commanded it to pull back into the clouds and be gone. There was no fear or doubt on my part, and the tornado obeyed instantly. From Bible study, I knew I possessed authority over the weather. The faith to remove that storm hinged on knowledge of the Lord's Word already in my spirit. The power released came through the gift of enlarging my faith to the capacity necessary.

4. *Healing*

The gift of healing turns the recipient into a donor. A person with this gift will actually be a vessel through which the Lord will pour His power to heal someone else's physical body without natural aids (such as the boy mentioned above under the word of knowledge).

5. *Miracles*

This gift also turns the believer into a "transmitter" of God's power to meet a specific need. Such miracles defy all natural laws and can actually change the structure or course of nature itself. The dismissal of the tornado mentioned earlier was the gift of miracles in operation with the gift of faith.

6. *Discerning Of Spirits*

This gift enables the believer to know with certainty the origin of the spirit behind certain behaviors or actions. It is quite often employed to discern demonic activity but can be used to confirm the presence and will of God in a situation. When referring to a demonic force, the actual name of the spirit may be given; at other times, it may simply be a yes or no discernment of what the source of the activity is.

A few years ago a man came to our church, and from his talk he sounded very spiritual. My spirit, however, was never comfortable when I was around him. Many people thought he was a great humanitarian and servant, but I could not buy it. Within a few weeks after his arrival, he began to spawn much hurt and division among our congregation. Eventually, he was asked to leave because he would not submit to the eldership. My uneasiness was a form of discerning of spirits. The man was not motivated by the Lord but by spirits of greed and lust for power. The Holy Spirit revealed this to me to confirm what was eventually brought to light.

7. *Tongues*

The gift of tongues is given to a believer for use in a specific instance to bring a message to the church or an individual. It is a language the believer has never learned and does not understand, even when he speaks it. This is not to be confused with the prayer language given to believers when they receive the Baptism in the Holy Spirit. That is a personal form of tongues, which can be utilized by a believer at any moment without specific unction from the Holy Spirit. The gift of tongues mentioned in 1 Corinthians chapter twelve is a specific urging of the Holy Spirit for a specific reason at a specific moment.

8. *Interpretation*

This gift is given that one might interpret a message given in tongues into the language of those present. Paul clearly stated in 1 Corinthians chapter fourteen that tongues without interpretation does the Body of Christ no good, even though it will edify the person who spoke merely because of their obedience. This interpretation will immediately follow the tongues given and may come through the same person who spoke the message in tongues, although that will not always be the case.

9. *Prophecy*

The gift of prophecy is given to a believer to bring a specific word from the Lord concerning specific matters. It may be directive, corrective, exhortive, or comforting.

Motivational Gifts
(Romans 12; 1 Corinthians 12)

The second gift category we will look at is that of motivational gifts. These are the gifts that spur Christians to action, usually in a service-oriented way. Motivational gifts tend to function on a daily basis rather than at specific moments directed by the Holy Ghost. Every believer will have one or more of these gifts operating in their lives at one time or another. To list these motivational gifts we must look at the twelfth chapter of Romans and 1 Corinthians chapter twelve. From the reference in Romans we find the following gifts.

1. *Prophecy*

This gift is not to be confused with the Holy Spirit gift of prophecy. While the Holy Spirit gift mentioned in 1 Corinthians chapter twelve is bestowed for specific instances to whomever the Spirit dictates, the motivational gift of prophecy is an ongoing gift. As part of the person's personality, it is the ability to see into a situation or person and bring forth an utterance from the Lord that pertains to a need or problem. The person with this gift may not necessarily be a prophet, yet they will most likely exhibit the attributes of one while delivering such a word.

2. *Service*

This gift motivates the believer to serve his brethren in various practical ways. These people will always be the ones cleaning up after a church function or taking food to the needy. They are seemingly driven to serve in some way or another and are only happy when doing so.

3. *Teaching*

The gift of teaching causes the believer to be constantly looking for the exactness of truth in God's Word so he may share it with the Body of Christ. His desire is to present the pure Word of God to benefit the Church. The longing to place things in a precept by precept, point by point outline is a good indication of this gift.

4. *Exhortation*

A person with the gift of exhortation will lift up and comfort, excite, and motivate the Body of Christ. Believers with this gift will constantly be edifying others and encouraging them to do great things for God!

5. *Giving*

This gift motivates believers to give of their natural and material resources for the benefit of others. They enjoy giving in every area and desire to move others to do so. Quite often these people are adept at producing or raising finances for specific ministries or needs.

6. *Leadership*

The gift of leadership causes the believer to organize and set goals of others and then direct those people to the accomplishment of those goals. This person will "keep the ball rolling" and help everyone work together toward the common end.

7. *Mercy*

This gift will move the believer with compassion and empathy toward those in great personal distress. They will perform the necessary tasks to help those hurting ones find relief. These people are very loving and self-sacrificing.

Following are the motivational gifts itemized in 1 Corinthians chapter twelve. (I have omitted those gifts already mentioned or that will come under the next category.)

8. *Helps*

The gift of helps motivates the believer to pour his time, efforts, gifts, and talents into the lives and ministries of others. They seek to assist someone else rather than themselves. The majority of believers are called to this gift, and all are to operate in it to some extent, even if just in their local church.

9. *Administrations*

This gift moves the believer much the same as that of leadership. The person with this gift will understand the goals—both short and long range—of a body and be involved in their execution at the leadership level.

Ministry Gifts
(Ephesians 4:11)

The third category of spiritual gifts is often called the five-fold ministry gifts. These gifts are given to believers called by God into full-time ministry. Although attributes of these gifts may be enjoyed by many believers, this gift category is for those with a lifetime call. These gifts, listed in Ephesians 4:11, are specifically given for the "equipping of the saints for the working of ministry" (4:12). Christians possessing these gifts are the trainers, coaches, and drill sergeants of God's army.

The majority of Christ's Body will *not* be found endowed with these special gifts. If all were trainers, there would be no army to send out for battle. All believers, however, should have a knowledge of these five gifts so they can submit to and receive from anointed ministers. These godly men and women have been appointed to build up the Body of Christ and help all participate in performing the Lord's perfect will.

1. *Apostle*

An apostle is an authoritative figure over the general church body rather than over one specific church. This person will both establish and oversee the spiritual workings of a local body and be a contributing factor in its leader's actions. The apostle is a strength to the entire Church, having an overall view and understanding of the Lord's work and will throughout His universal Body.

2. *Prophet*

This gift allows the believer to be the voice of God to the people. He will have the ability to connect present situations to the perfect will of God. The gift of prophecy will operate in his ministry with one hundred percent accuracy. He will speak in a way that will convict as well as edify. A prophet will tell of future events concerning the Church as well as reveal the meaning of past and present events. His attitude will be one of absolute submission to God by all.

3. *Evangelist*

This gift allows the believer to share the gospel with people under an anointing of God that often brings conviction and conversion to the hearers. The evangelist will be successful at leading many to salvation in one-on-one and possibly in mass meeting situations. He will be consumed by the desire to tell people about Christ and to train and exhort others to do the same.

4. *Pastor*

A pastor will become a shepherd to a certain group of brethren. He will have a feel and concern for the needs of his church at any given moment and will help teach, comfort, direct, and correct them to meet those needs. This is usually a long-range position lived out with one church body.

5. *Teacher*

This gift enables the believer to acquire and then share in-depth truths of the Bible with the church in a systematic and logical course. His goal will be to see that those listening to him both learn and apply what he teaches. He will delight in using every available circumstance as a tool or example to share a biblical truth with anyone who will listen.

Investing

Each of us has received one or more of the gifts listed in this chapter (with the exception of the ones listed under Holy Spirit gifts, for they will be at the discretion of the Lord for the specific time and event He so desires). But as with anything given us freely by the Lord, we must accept responsibility for its exercise and produce fruit thereby. The Gospel of Matthew contains a graphic illustration of this mandate. God wants us to have an understanding of His spiritual gifts, as noted in 1 Corinthians 12:1: "Now concerning spiritual gifts, brethren, I do not want you to be unaware." Not only that, He expects us to cultivate a *desire* for them, actually striving to operate in those considered greater than other gifts. (See 1 Corinthians 12:31; 1 Corinthians 14:1.)

Our Heavenly Father even takes the point a step further by prodding us to "stir up" or rekindle the gifts within us that may have become dormant for any reason. (See 2 Timothy 1:6.) And just in case there is a hardhead in the camp (such as yours truly), 1 Timothy 4:14 contains the emphatic order exhorting us to be sure that neglect of our gifts is never an option. As explained in these few verses, which are sprinkled across the epistles, the responsibility for using our gifts, be they spiritual or natural, quite plainly lies with us.

Think about it. What giver is held responsible for the gift once it has been given? But also, what giver isn't frustrated when a gift is unemployed by the recipient? Clearly, the Father trusts His children to be "good stewards."

Do we deserve such trust? I think not. For as Romans 12:6 instructs, it is God's grace that determines the gifts we receive. This truth should spur us on, all the more, to excellence in the use of our gifts. God's grace was anything but cheap to Jesus Christ. The price of His death alone is justification enough for the magnitude of consequence He places on those unwilling to use what He has imparted.

As we discover in this example, there are serious consequences for one who allows these gifts to lay idle:

> "For it is just like a man about to go on a journey, who called his own slaves, and entrusted his possessions to them. And to one he gave five talents, to another, two, and to another, one, each according to his own ability; and he went on his journey. Immediately the one who had received the five talents went and traded with them, and gained five more talents. In the same manner the one who had received the two talents gained two more. But he who received the one talent went away and dug in the ground, and hid his master's money.

"Now after a long time the master of those slaves came and settled accounts with them. And the one who had received the five talents came up and brought five more talents, saying, 'Master, you entrusted five talents to me; see, I have gained five more talents.' His master said to him, 'Well done, good and faithful slave; you were faithful with a few things, I will put you in charge of many things, enter into the joy of your master.'

"The one also who had received the two talents came up and said, 'Master, you entrusted to me two talents; see, I have gained two more talents.' His master said to him, 'Well done, good and faithful slave; you were faithful with a few things, I will put you in charge of many things; enter into the joy of your master.'

"And the one also who had received the one talent came up and said, 'Master, I knew you to be a hard man, reaping where you did not sow, and gathering where you scattered no seed. And I was afraid, and went away and hid your talent in the ground; see, you have what is yours.' But his master answered and said to him, 'You wicked, lazy slave, you knew that I reap where I did not sow, and gather where I scattered no seed. Then you ought to have put my money in the bank, and on my arrival I would have received my money back with interest. Therefore take away the talent from him, and give it to the one who has the ten talents.'

"For everyone who has shall more be given, and he shall have an abundance; but from the one who does not have, even what he does have shall be taken away. And cast out the worthless slave into the outer darkness; in that place there shall be weeping and gnashing of teeth'—Matthew 25:14-30.

This parable illustrates a powerful principle we must apply to our spiritual gift. It is not the number of gifts we possess that determines our reward but what we *do* with what we are given. If we are faithful to achieve our utmost with our gift, then there will be a reward for us. In fact, equal blessing was given to the two "faithful" servants, even though their initial gifts and increases were quite different. It is the person who does nothing with the gift granted to him that will be found wanting.

So, if we fail to utilize our gift for the Kingdom of God, we may not even enjoy the *possibility* of its use. According to Christ's teaching, to bury that gift is a serious offense.

An easy parallel to this principle of gift invest-ment and return can be found in the training of circus performers. I may have trained for years to acquire the skill necessary to climb a ladder on a slackwire, but a lack of practice can take its toll quite suddenly. A misplaced step or an overcom-pensation in balance can prove disasterous, to say the least. My skills must be kept sharp through investing time in rigorous practice sessions. Just as any athlete's abilities begin to atrophy from lack of persistent training, so our spiritual gifts can wane.

Through this parable, the Lord sets a strong standard for those who would walk with Him. However, that standard is both attainable and worth the effort. The cost versus the benefit is, once again, in our favor. Notice that the money was never the property of the servants, only their responsibility. But upon their proper stewardship of that responsibility, they were rewarded with not only greater opportunities for faithfulness, but the money of their fellow servant was given to them as well. The Lord never fails to reward the faithful.

The gifts the Lord has endowed you with are for His glory and for meeting the needs of His Body. As each of us finds our specific gifts and begins to live them out on a daily basis, the Church will be strengthened, and the world will be forced to take notice.

These gifts are for giving away. They are for use by each of us to assist us in our purpose in life.

As we strive to find and develop our purpose, our spiritual and natural gifts will come more and more into play to bring about its fulfillment. You *are* gifted!

During my study of spiritual gifts, I have come to understand the heartbeat of Paul's longing to impart such spiritual gifts to the church in Rome. His desire wasn't so much the gift itself but that through the gift those believers would be established. (See Romans 1:11.) The learned apostle understood that the person who was in step with the gifts of God's Spirit would be firmly set in a position of victory.

This is my prayer for you as well. For isn't the hand established in the body due to its unique abilities—likewise, the eye, the ear, and the heart? Every member of our human body is established by its special skill, firmly set in place, proven, and, of course, much needed.

When you, as a believer, discover and begin to live within the realm of the gifts God has entrusted to you, you will, likewise, be established within His Body. Through those gifts you will be utilizing the very power of God to live out your particular purpose, thereby enhancing the overall purpose of not only your local church but the Body of Christ at large.

Suggested reading:

1. Hickey, Marilyn. *Motivational Gifts*. Dallas: Word of Faith Publishing, 1983.

2. Wagner, Peter. *Your Spiritual Gifts Can Help Your Church Grow*. Ventura: Regal Books, 1979.

4

FIND IT!

Seeking the Kingdom of God is a command, not an option: "But seek first His *kingdom* and His righteousness; and all these things shall be added to you" (Matthew 6:33, *Italics added*). If the Lord has a vision and plan for your life, then it must be within the realm of His Kingdom. (See Figure 2-B.)

I do not believe God would have any of His precious children operating outside of His Kingdom. Anything outside of the Kingdom of God is in the kingdom of Satan. According to Colossians 1:13, we have been delivered from Satan's kingdom into the Kingdom of God's beloved Son.

We are *in* the world (Satan's) but not *of* it. As Christians, our actions help destroy the enemy's strongholds. (See 2 Corinthians 10:4.) This obviously refers to both our God-ordained purpose and our day-to-day Christian activity.

Assuming that you agree that the vision and plan ordained for you by God is within the confines

65

of His Kingdom, let's discover its location. Once that location has been established, we can then begin the task of transferring your vision from His Kingdom into this natural world, where you will live it out.

Jesus states in Luke 17:21, "Nor will they say, 'Look here it is!' or 'There it is!' For behold, the kingdom of God is in your midst." The *King James Version* says, "The Kingdom of God is within you."

The Lord explains here that the Kingdom of God is inside each one of us who calls Jesus "Lord." This can be easily understood by realizing that a king always lives within the borders of his kingdom. (Absentee kingship never has proved a very worthwhile or long-lived state of authority.)

When a person receives Christ as Lord, He comes to live inside their spirit. Therefore, it is logical to assume that if Christ lives inside us, His Kingdom must be inside us. Our lives become the borders of His Kingdom. If our vision is inside God's Kingdom, and His Kingdom is inside us, then our vision is inside us. (See Figure 2-C.) *The God-ordained purpose for your life, the entire vision God has for you is inside you already! It is lodged in your spirit because that is where the Kingdom of God resides.*

Your vision is a seed, and God's Kingdom is the shell in which it is tightly, yet lovingly, held. But a vision locked up inside the Kingdom of God within you will be worthless. Neither you, the

66

unsaved world, His Church, nor the Lord Himself will ever receive its benefits. You must find the keys to release it.

The Revealer

We said in the first chapter that when we receive a personal vision, a *revealed* word from God, it will restrain or guide us. The Holy Spirit of God will reveal our vision to us so the vision can lead and guide us:

> "For when He, *the Spirit of truth,* comes, *He* will *guide* you into all the truth; for *He* will not speak on His own initiative, but whatever *He* hears, *He* will speak; and He *will disclose to you* what is to come. *He* shall glorify Me; for *He* shall take of Mine, and shall *disclose it to you.* All things that the Father has are Mine; therefore I said, that *He* takes of Mine, and will disclose to you"—John 16:13-15, *Italics added.*

We are clearly instructed here that the Holy Spirit will reveal to us *all* that is the Father's. All means "all inclusive." Such revealing must, therefore, include our personal purpose and vision! The Holy Spirit will open to us the plan our Father in heaven has ordained for us.

The Language Of The Spirit

The Lord uttered a comforting, yet often frustrating, promise when he proclaimed, "My sheep hear My voice, and I know them, and they follow Me" (John 10:27). Jesus comforts us by factually stating that we as His sheep *do* hear His voice. His declaration that we will also follow Him implies that we will understand His words when He does speak to us. Herein lies the agonizing frustration of many believers—hearing and understanding so we may follow correctly.

Most of us believe we can hear the Lord's voice; we're just not sure which voice is His. Is it Jesus, us, the devil, or the pizza we ate last night? To assist us in putting an end to such nerve-racking questions, the Lord set down the laws cited above concerning the Holy Spirit as the Revealer of God's will. It is the Holy Spirit's job to speak to us in a way that we can hear, understand, and follow. Our job is to learn and listen to His communication.

In order to accomplish this, the Holy Spirit created His own unique language—a language composed of thoughts, ideas, visions, and dreams. He will plant them as seeds within the fertile soil of your spirit and mind. However, if you do not understand the language of the Holy Spirit, you will not hear and therefore will not be able to obey Him when He begins to reveal God's purpose or any other command to you.

To become a successful circus performer, I was forced to learn the unique language of the circus. Until I knew the names of the various pieces of rigging and the meaning of specific commands, it was virtually impossible for me to progress in the circus realm. As an unlearned beginner, I committed many errors due to my ignorance of the language. When someone asked me to "take a foot on that block and set a bite," I was helpless to obey. It was most frustrating for all involved. Not only was I continually embarrassed by missed assignments, but my coaches and fellow troupe members were also often hindered in their efforts. When I learned the language, however, I became capable of understanding instructions and carrying them out.

The parallel to our individual purpose should be obvious. If we don't understand the language of the Holy Spirit, we block both our own lives and the overall plan of the Lord's Church. We must acquire the exciting, revealing language of the Holy Spirit in order to accomplish our assigned tasks as individuals, thereby advancing the master work of God's people as well.

God's Word lists over two hundred and thirty instances in which the Lord spoke to His people through visions and dreams. In thirty-two separate books of the Bible, these visions and dreams are detailed, with fourteen such occurrences in the book of Acts alone. In fact, the entire last book of the Bible, the Revelation, is all *one* vision.

This extraordinary language was used constantly to communicate God's purpose and plan for individuals and His people as a nation.

We are not only speaking of those dreams and visions you experience while you are asleep. Neither are we limiting the term "vision" to awesome angelic appearances. These visions and dreams include God-inspired thoughts and ideas. The Holy Spirit will skillfully insert His Words and thoughts into your mind. You may never hear an audible voice. Most people never do. But daily, at any moment, God can flash His ideas across your brain. Thousands of images a day flow through the average person's mind. It would be ridiculous to think that God would not be a part of those ideas and thoughts. Throughout His Word, He proves again and again that it is a major avenue of His guidance for His people.

Jesus was led in this way during His life on earth. He was guided by the Father on a moment-by-moment basis, for He proclaimed,

> "Truly, truly, I say to you, the Son can do nothing of Himself, unless it is something He *sees* the Father doing; for whatever the Father does, these things the Son also does *in like manner.* For the Father loves the Son, and *shows* Him all things that He Himself is doing; and greater works than these will He *show* Him, that you may marvel. . . . I can do

70

nothing on My own initiative. As I *hear,* I judge; and My judgment is just, because I do not seek My own will, but the will of Him who sent Me"—John 5:19-20, 30, *Italics added.*

Jesus was so in tune with the Father that He was able to receive the most exact instructions and never miss once, in seeing, hearing, or doing. These instructions probably came through the thoughts and ideas Christ received during His time of prayer, rather than supernatural visions or voices. The New Testament only records one open vision that Jesus experienced. That vision was on the Mount of Transfiguration, when He was engulfed in the shining white glory of God as He conversed with Elijah and Moses. (I am not saying that God did not give Jesus other visions and dreams, but that is the only recorded vision.)

The Bible records two times that the Father spoke audibly during Jesus' human life, yet both were merely to confirm the fact of Christ's Sonship—a fact Jesus was well aware of already. With this in mind, it is safe to assume that the Father spoke to Jesus through His thoughts—through His spirit (His inner man).

For example, how did Jesus know it was time to be baptized by John? Or by what means of communication did the Holy Spirit lead Him into the desert to be tempted? I believe it was through thoughts and ideas flowing across His mind. Many times in Scripture we are told that Jesus departed to a lonely place to pray. When He would come down from the mountain or up from the desert after those times of prayer, He would perform great miracles. Why? Because during those seasons of communication with the heavenly Father, more of the purpose for Christ's life was revealed. God would speak to Him in the thoughts and images of His mind.

In John 12:49, Jesus stated that He did not speak on His own initiative but that His words were given Him by God. How did those words come to Him? They came by thoughts and ideas crossing His mind. The Holy Spirit will speak to us in like manner concerning the vision, purpose, and plan that He has for our lives, thus fulfilling Jesus' promise of our doing the works He did and giving hope for the promise of greater works. (See John 14:12.)

I believe such inner guidance is a much higher form of receptiveness than physical communication from the Father—hearing an audible voice, etc. The ability to discern God's still, small voice with clarity and confidence is the result of a solid relationship between sender and receiver. (See 1 Kings 19:12.) It requires a deep, meaningful life of faith. Jesus obviously possessed such faith.

Remember, also, that "vision" means *mental sight*. Many times the Holy Spirit will show you the actual images of those things He wants you to do. (Look again at John 5:19-20, and notice that

72

the word "show" is used twice in conjunction with Christ's submission to the Father's will.) A thought will come as a picture. Actually, all thoughts are mental pictures of something, even if just the words themselves. The Holy Spirit plants pictures within us as He communicates God's will.

I believe the Father did this for Jesus on a constant basis. Jesus always spoke the *answers* to a problem—the finished product—instead of the problem or its steps to completion. The Father gave Jesus mental sight of the completed picture of His will. Be it healing a paralytic or raising the dead, Jesus "saw" the answer. If Jesus is our example, it is reasonable to believe that God will do the same for us.

Listening To The Spirit

Over the past several years, I have grown accustomed to listening carefully to the wonderful language of the Holy Spirit. When I pray, I am actually surprised if He does not share with me a vision, a thought, or a mental image of some sort. As I intercede for someone, I do so fully expecting the Holy Spirit to reveal to me, through His language, precisely how to meet the need. After all, He knows exactly what must be done. The Father desires to work through His children, of which I am one, so I should well expect Him to communicate the solution to me. That's not arrogance—it's Bible. And it works!

For instance, once I was praying for a young woman. She came to me and pleaded, "I need direction in my life." As I began to pray for her, I saw a picture in my mind of that woman sitting in a large wing-back chair, hunched over an old, dark, stained wooden desk. Standing in the upper right hand corner of the desk was a tiny brass lamp with a delicate milkglass shade. The woman was writing busily in a large, black covered three-ring notebook. There were several other such notebooks cluttering the desk's well-worn top. In the deep-grey background of that dimly lit room I could see a silver haired old woman wrapped in a large-knit shawl sitting silently in an old rocking chair.

As the image disappeared, I realized that this was the Holy Spirit speaking to me about the direction He had for this woman's life. I interpreted the vision as the Holy Spirit inspired it to me and told her what I had seen. The interpretation was, "Whatever you were writing in that notebook, whatever you were working on at that moment, and whoever that woman in the background is, *that* is your direction."

Her eyes widened as she listened to me speak. Then, somewhat awestruck, she related to me that just the night before she had been at a relative's house working at the very desk I had described. She had been studying and formulating plans to help her elderly grandmother, who was actually sitting in that room behind her as she wrote.

God had shown me, through the language of the Holy Spirit (which is thoughts and visions), exactly what that woman had been doing the night before! She then acknowledged, "I have always had a desire to help old people." I assured her that this desire was part of the Lord's direction for her life. The anxiety on her face suddenly lifted and was replaced by a noticeable expression of peace.

The Lord states again and again that He shows no partiality toward His people and will give us *all* that He has given to Christ. If Jesus knew the language of the Holy Spirit, then you and I also have that privilege. But we must strive daily to develop this divine form of communication. It demands much time spent in prayer and worship of our Lord. It will require sacrifice. But the reward of such time and sacrifice is the priceless ability to be led and guided by the Creator of all. The cost versus the benefit is definitely in our favor!

From Seed To Fruition

Take a moment now and look about the room you are seated in. Every object you see, even the book that you now hold in your hand, began as a mere idea—an inspired thought in someone's attentive mind. That thought or mental picture eventually became the physical reality that you now experience. However, that idea did not simply leap from their mind to instant physical reality. Instead, the idea underwent many phases

75

of development before it materialized. Your own purpose will also be revealed and lived out in a step-by-step process. The steps of that process are in you right now.

When the Father reveals His vision for your life to you, it will begin as one simple yet powerful thought or idea. That thought or idea is like a seed, having within it the entire plan for what it represents. In every acorn is the plan for a mighty oak tree. Each kernel of corn holds the potential to become a stalk with many ears. Likewise, when God conceives the seed of your purpose in the womb of your spirit and mind, it will contain the complete plan for its achievement. Those detailed plans will be revealed to you continually in the same manner as the first thought or idea—by the picturesque language of the Holy Spirit.

5

CONFIRMING YOUR VISION

Once you begin to recognize the voice of the Holy Spirit, understand His language, and receive the vision He has for your life, you must then confirm beyond a shadow of a doubt that what you are receiving is actually His instruction. Your enemy, the devil, will attempt to confuse and distract you. Friends and loved ones may not believe in your dream. Even your own thoughts, imaginings, and ideas can rise up with doubts and fears against you. Therefore, to assist you in realizing your true purpose and vision, the Lord has established within His Word several ways in which we may confirm His leading.

Before any of these points of confirmation should be enlisted, your total commitment to the Lord and His will for your life must be affirmed. You must be confident of a solid relationship with your heavenly Father. Such a relationship will require much time spent with Him in prayer, Bible study, fellowship with other Christians, and witnessing to those who have not heard about Christ. You *must* establish your relationship with the Lord before He can confirm His will to you. The more deeply you root that relationship, the more easily you will hear and understand the Holy Spirit's language and receive His leading.

Let me illustrate this. I have three children. When each was born, they were no more aware of me than anyone else. They recognized neither my voice nor the touch of my hand. But as I spent time with them, they heard my voice, felt my touch, and saw my face over and over. Eventually, our relationship was established. When I spoke or simply entered the nursery, they instantly responded to me. Now, after several years of such constant interaction, we can express our love for one another in two-way communication. The relationship I now have with my children was built upon the foundation of consistent, daily contact.

So it is with our heavenly Father. We must take the time to build that relationship, for if it has not been properly secured, then clear communication with God will not be ours. Without such clarity, the following points of confirmation will be difficult for us to use.

If you are a person who has yet to establish such a relationship with the Lord, I suggest that before you proceed with this chapter you make the decision to do so. Only a truly committed believer will adhere to the following points of confirmation, for they will require a self-motivated patience.

Hearing and following the voice of our Lord can be simultaneously the most exciting and nerve frazzling exercise of our Christian lives. The fear of "missing" God on any given instruction can paralyze the strongest disciple. But Jesus did not come to bind those desiring to do His will. Instead, He came to free the captive.

God has a will for you, which He reveals by His Spirit. By utilizing the following points of confirmation, you will be capable of attaining freedom from the binding chains of fear. Rest assured He will dispel all of your doubts when He shows you His plan.

1. *Prayer*

In Matthew 6:5-7 we read,

> "And when you pray, you are not to
> be as hypocrites; for they love to stand
> on the street corners, in order to be seen
> by men. Truly I say to you, they have
> their reward in full. But you, *when you
> pray,* go into your inner room, and
> when you have *shut your door,* pray to
> your Father who is *in secret,* and your
> Father who sees in secret will repay you.
> And when you are praying, *do not
> use meaningless repetition,* as the

Gentiles do, for they suppose that they will be heard for their many words''— *Italics added*.

Jesus was laying the foundation for personal prayer. He explained that *when* we pray (not if), we should walk into our closet and shut the door behind us. We should speak to the Lord in secret, and, if we do so, He will reward us outside the closet. One of the ways in which God will reward His children is through a greater ability to hear His voice and live out His instructions. My time in prayer is often my greatest time of inspiration and the most productive time of communication with the Holy Spirit. It was during such times of communion with God that I began to understand His language and establish an unshakable relationship with my Father.

When the Lord reveals to you your purpose in life, He will confirm it during such times of prayer. He will communicate to you whether or not it is His vision by the thoughts in your spirit and mind. In John 10:27, Jesus made the statement that God's sheep will hear His voice and follow Him. *We* are His sheep, and we *will* know His voice if we learn to listen for it. This means we must take time during our daily prayer sessions to *listen* for His words in our mind and spirit. We should not be rude and monopolize the conversation but instead sit quietly and listen so He may speak His will. He is our Father. If we truly love Him, as we say we do, then we must listen so we can obey. Prayer must be a two-way channel if we are to receive our confirmation clearly.

2. *Inner Peace*

Galatians 5:22 states, "But the fruit of the Spirit is love, joy, peace, patience, kindness, goodness, faithfulness." We see here that peace is a part of the fruit of the Spirit. If God is giving you a vision or a dream or revealing your purpose to you, He will always confirm it with a feeling of peace within you. When you think about the vision or dream—when you dwell on it or daydream about it—you have a peaceful feeling inside. If it is not from God, there will be a scratchy feeling—an uneasy restlessness about the entire idea.

Remember this point when you are confirming your vision or anything from the Lord. If there is no peace, don't move toward that goal. This is often referred to as the witness of the Holy Spirit. Where the Spirit of the Lord is, *there* is peace.

3. *The Word Of God*

In Psalm 119:105 we read, "Thy word is a lamp to my feet, and a light to my path."

Second Timothy 3:16 says, "All Scripture is inspired by God and profitable for teaching, for reproof, for correction, for training in righteousness."

These two verses explain that God's Word is both a light for our search of direction and a tool to train us in the areas needed to accomplish our goals. Our Father in heaven not only desires to illuminate our path, but He wants to equip us for the journey as well. His Word is more than able to handle both tasks.

Please understand that the vision God gives you will never contradict the Bible but will always be in line with it. There are three methods the Father may utilize to confirm His will to you through His Word.

A. You may be reading the Bible one day when *a verse will seem to leap off the page at you.* It will almost stand up on the page. You won't be able to leave that verse and may read it over and over again. This is one avenue God may use to confirm His vision to you. When a verse seems to jump out at you in this way and is in line with the vision you feel you have received from the Lord, it will be a point of confirmation.

B. Repetition is a common means used by the Holy Spirit to confirm certain items to believers. Several times in one day the exact same Bible verse pertaining to your vision may come across your path. It may be spoken by a friend, read in a book, heard on the radio, or found in the Bible itself during daily reading. Such constant occurrence of the same scripture many times is the Lord confirming to us that the visions we are dwelling on are from Him.

C. Another way the Lord may use His Word to confirm a thought or idea is by the Holy Spirit *dropping Scripture references into your mind.* Many times as I have prayed over certain ideas I felt were of God, several references have entered my mind in rapid succession. Whenever this happens, I write them down and immediately look them up. Quite often these verses point toward or away from my idea, depending on whether or not God is the author of that idea. (He can also give scriptures to let you know your idea or vision is *not* His will.)

One thing you can be sure of is that if a vision *is* from the Lord, He will *always* confirm it by His Word.

4. *Wise Counsel*

> The way of a fool is right in his own eyes, but a wise man is he who listens to counsel—Proverbs 12:15.
> Through presumption comes nothing but strife, but with those who receive counsel is wisdom—Proverbs 13:10.
> Without consultation, plans are frustrated, but with many counselors they succeed—Proverbs 15:22.

Success is guaranteed when you enlist wise counsel. The key word here is *wise.* Someone who is a wise counselor is a person experienced in the area you are discussing with him. If you need wise counsel in a financial matter, you talk to someone with expertise in money matters. If you need wise counsel in automobiles, you should approach someone experienced in that area.

The finest counsel of all is the counsel of the Lord. Proverbs 19:21 promises us that His counsel will stand. This being true, it is always best to seek godly people for wise counsel. Your first such counselors should be your pastor and elders in the local body to which you are committed. These men are specifically anointed by God to help direct your Christian life. Their knowledge of your personal life will be a valuable resource.

Concerning a vision God has planted within your heart, always seek godly people who have experience in the area of that vision. You can be assured, based on these scriptures, that the Lord will share much confirmation with you through godly, wise counselors.

5. *Circumstance*

The Lord will manipulate and control natural circumstances to confirm His Word—His revelation to you. Through everyday happenings in your life, the Lord can create crystal clear direction toward or away from your vision. Many Christians often refer to the cliche, ''The Lord seemed to open the door,'' when referring to guidance on a certain item. This *is* a Bible-based idiom yet a dangerous one if given total obedience without seeking and receiving any other means of confirmation.

The reference to "opened" or "closed" doors comes from the apostle Paul's mention of it in 1 Corinthians 16:8-9: "But I shall remain in Ephesus until Pentecost; for a wide door for effective service has opened to me, and there are many adversaries."

Obviously certain circumstances directed that evangelism was in season in Ephesus, and Paul meant to harvest some souls. But to think that Paul was acting solely on such circumstance would be ignorant on our part. The apostle had many years of missionary work under his belt and was well versed in the guidance of God's Holy Spirit. In fact, in this same letter he teaches on the supernatural gifts of the Lord and the master plan He has for the Church—each member specifically placed. Paul did not base his actions on open doors alone, and neither should we.

Let me share a personal example with you. My wife, Meg, and I were seeking confirmation whether or not to buy a certain house. During our time of seeking that confirmation, several key circumstances fell into place that pointed toward a direct confirmation of the word we felt God was giving us to buy the house.

One circumstance was that the owner of the house we were then renting wanted to move back into the house on a certain date. That date was directly in line with the time we could move into the house we desired to purchase. Another circumstance was the amount the seller required as a down payment. It was almost the exact amount we had just received from an inheritance. These circumstances, although quite convincing, were *not* the deciding factor in buying that house. We considered these as only part of the confirmation we sought.

Circumstances should *never* be employed as the only means of direction or confirmation. By applying circumstances as your sole means of confirming a word from the Lord, you may find yourself like a pinball bouncing from circumstance to circumstance, never really attaining the goal the Father has set before you. A pinball is directed by whatever it encounters. Led and guided *completely* by its circumstances, it actually has no direction at all and accomplishes nothing. Many Christians operate in such haphazard ways, devoid of divine guidance. In order to avoid the pinball trap, trust circumstances only *in conjunction with* the other points of confirmation discussed here.

6. *Supernatural Happenings*

God uses the supernatural. He will use open visions, and He will use dreams. He will appear to people or have His angels appear to people. God can speak in an audible voice from the clouds or out of a burning bush. He can speak through prophesies, animals, and storms. Our heavenly Father can cause oceans to part and trees to wither. He is a supernatural God.

As a pastor and elder at my home church, and as a traveling evangelist/teacher, I have been both thrilled and shocked by the use and abuse of the gift of prophecy. Many wonderful words of direction have been given by God through anointed saints, and much good has been done. I have marvelled at utterances of young and old alike.

But many times I have sat heartbroken as I listened to the tears of those destroyed by a "personal" prophecy that they followed to the letter, only to be blown out of the water by an enemy torpedo. By taking "a word" from a well-meaning brother or sister, they ran headlong into the snare of the devil. No prophecy should ever be lived out without the guidance and confirmation of a spiritually mature leader beforehand.

First Corinthians 14:29 admonishes us to judge prophecies. Taking a "prophecy" unchecked can prove disasterous, but one tested and approved by godly leadership will prove prosperous. Be alert as to the spiritual maturity of the one prophesying. Although any believer can be used by God to share a word of prophecy, it is a good and safe rule to receive such from a proven spiritual leader. Seek godly confirmation on supernatural utterances.

Again and again throughout the Bible God used supernatural happenings to lead, guide, and confirm His Word and will for His people. He can and may do the same with you. However, I caution you again: do not use supernatural happenings as a sole means of confirming the vision and ideas God may plant within you. First, because the Bible states that Satan himself can appear as an angel of light. Many brethren have been deceived in this way. (See 2 Corinthians 11:14; 4:4.) Second, such happenings are rare when compared to the total time span of Bible history. Thousands of years have recorded only hundreds of occurrences among millions of believers. Always make sure supernatural manifestations are not your only means of confirming the word you feel God is speaking to you.

7. *God's Timing*

When all six of the above points are in agreement, you can be sure God has spoken to you to confirm the word that He has revealed to your heart. But if you launch out before His perfect time dictates, you can fail miserably. You must see to it, when you confirm your vision, that you continue to seek Him concerning the correct moment for stepping out and acting on that vision.

Remember, it is the Holy Spirit's duty to lead you and guide you in *all* truth. All truth includes God's exact timing. He will reveal it to you, and again it will come through His language of visions, dreams, thoughts, and ideas. For many, including myself, this point can be the most difficult to wait for the Lord to reveal. Our zeal often overpowers our patience. Too many plans have fallen short of the mark due to either haste or tardiness. God has a perfect time for your dream. Find it and follow it.

Let me illustrate the importance of this seventh point. When my wife and I bought the house mentioned earlier, we had much work to finish on it. After we moved in, the pressure to complete the work created a good deal of friction between us. It seemed as though we would never get it all done. My wife, Meg, began to ask, "Do you think we heard from God? Should we have done this?"

Immediately we thought back to these seven points of confirmation. As we discussed each point, the confirmations seemed crystal clear, until we got to the timing. We suddenly realized that we had never sought the Lord's will in that area. As we did so over the next few days, He revealed that we had been premature in the purchase of our home. He had wanted us to give a portion of our inheritance money toward our pledge for our church building fund. By giving to the Lord's work first, we would not have had enough for our down payment on the house. The time needed for God to bring in the balance of the down payment, however, would have allowed the builder to complete the house, and we never would have experienced the anxiety of doing the work ourselves.

It was a costly error, to be sure. Not only did we endure the pressure of finishing our home but also the distress of not paying off our commitment to the building fund on time. This was not the ideal method of learning the lesson of God's timing, but it was one we will never forget.

These seven confirmation points can deliver commanding peace in the midst of the storms that may rage against us. Knowing beyond a shadow of a doubt that the Lord has spoken His perfect will to you brings a bold confidence to the heart. I pray you will learn from our successes and failures mentioned here and utilize these points diligently and often in your quest to find your purpose in God's plan.

Fleeces And Lots

I wish to share two more points with you concerning guidance and confirmation of the vision God puts in your heart. These ideas concern "putting out a fleece" and "drawing lots." I mention these two confirmations with great caution, for even though both are biblical and seem effective, they can be extremely dangerous if used alone.

In Judges chapters six and seven, we read about Gideon, who used a fleece—a sheepskin—to test God concerning a certain vision. To make sure the Lord had spoken to him, Gideon laid the fleece on the ground one night and asked God to make the dew settle only on the fleece and not on the ground around it. The Lord did so. The next night Gideon tested God again, asking Him to have the dew rest only on the ground and leave the fleece completely dry. God also granted this request. Gideon took these supernatural occurrences as a sign that he had received orders from the Lord, and, acting upon that confirmation, he led Israel to victory in battle.

Drawing lots is found in Acts chapter one and was used to choose the apostle who would replace Judas Iscariot. The use of this method was probably based on Proverbs 16:33: "The lot is cast into the lap, but its every decision is from the Lord." The apostles prayed and asked the Lord to direct the drawing of the lots. When the lots were drawn, Matthias received the apostleship.

As I mentioned, both points of confirmation are biblically based and were effective. Both are dangerous, however, because they deal with supernatural happenings. You are asking the Lord to intervene supernaturally into your circumstances. This is an inferior form of guidance. You must remember that Satan can manipulate natural circumstances, too.

I once heard a story of a woman who "put out a fleece to the Lord" after hearing about Gideon's venture. She was not born again and had been receiving much petition from Christians to receive Christ as her Savior. She presented the "fleece" by stating she would accept the religion of the next person who came to her door. She was expecting God to send the correct one. That was her fleece.

The next person of any religious caliber who came to her door was from an anti-Christian cult!

That woman fell into the deception of Satan and involved herself in the cult. She had used a biblical principle, but because she was dealing with natural circumstances as her *only* means of communication, Satan was able to enter in and manipulate it.

As we study Gideon in Judges chapter six, we see that he had a weak relationship with God when he cast his fleece. In fact, in verse thirteen he even questioned whether God had His hand on Israel, let alone Gideon himself! This explains why the Lord honored the requests of Gideon as He did. Because there was little communication between Gideon and God, the Lord was almost forced to share with him in this supernatural way. Gideon is not the model of daily communion with the Father that we should imitate. His example of guidance and confirmation techniques is poor.

I don't ask my wife every morning to give me a sign that she is still my wife or that she will have supper ready for me when I come home from work. I *know* my wife. We communicate. We do not rely on signs and wonders to trust one another because we have developed our relationship beyond that point. When we first began dating, we used romantic niceties to impress upon each other the love we shared. Even though such signs and wonders are still in play in our lives, they are no longer necessary to convince each other of our feelings. Our relationship with the Father God should be as good and, in fact, even better.

We can also see in the book of Acts the real reason the apostles picked the new disciple by drawing straws. Because they had not established their spiritual relationship with the Lord to the point they could hear His voice within them, they were forced to use other avenues of communication. They required natural means to confirm the Word of God. Thus the drawing of lots.

After the day of Pentecost, however, the disciples no longer employed such means but relied on the language of the Holy Spirit, who spoke to their inner man to confirm God's direction. The prime example is given in chapter thirteen of the book of Acts, where Paul and Barnabas were called out by the Holy Spirit during a gathering of prophets and teachers as they ministered to God. There were no lots drawn or fleeces set out. The Word of the Lord came through the mouths of the prophets and teachers as they communed with God. Their relationship with the Lord had grown to the point that they could hear Him from within. Our relationship with the Almighty should ever be marching toward that goal.

I caution you: don't ''get fleeced'' or end up with ''the short end of the stick.'' Never use these two items as the sole means of guidance. I advise you to grow in your relationship with the Lord to the extent that you do not need such natural means to confirm His word to you but that you can trust the conviction and guidance of the Holy Spirit within you.

We have a Father who loves us dearly. He has a definite plan for our lives. To make sure we discover that plan, with the element of doubt removed, He devised the points of confirmation just listed. As we strive to utilize these points, they will become a strength and bulwark in our daily lives, not only for our overall purpose in life but for any instruction we feel God is sharing with us.

6

THE POWER OF THE WRITTEN WORD

No man or woman of God is called to a vision of survival only. Our purpose in this life will both meet the needs and require the assistance of other believers. Ours is the life of shared dreams and family interaction. To allow one another the opportunity to share in our visions, we must see to it that they are informed. As you may have already guessed, the Lord has some specific words on this matter.

Habakkuk 2:2 says, "Then the Lord answered me and said, 'Record the vision and inscribe it on tablets that the one who reads it may run.' " There are three main reasons why you should write down your vision. One, it will solidify to you that your vision is from the Lord. Two, it will help focus the details of that vision for you. Three, it will cause you to commit yourself to the vision. A force is linked to the written word that illuminates and sinks a vision deeply into your heart.

In Habakkuk, the Lord instructs His prophet to inscribe his vision on tablets made of stone. A message pounded into stone is permanent. A written vision will set a permanence within our hearts. You may attempt to cover it over or even run away from it, but once that vision has been written down, God will see to it that your deepest desire is to run with it.

Our heavenly Father takes no pleasure in the single-handed visionary. He delights in shoulder to shoulder workmanship. The verse from Habakkuk alludes to others who will read the vision that you write down and take up the race with you. The margin of the *New American Standard Bible* states that the runner who reads the vision should be able to do so fluently, with ease of understanding.

Participants in a race must know in advance the course they are to run. Without such information, they would not know where to start the race, where to finish it, or the correct route in between. If the race director simply explained to the runners, "This race will go from Los Angeles to New York and back," their first question would be, "What is the route?" He might describe the route in detail, but after a few miles it would be forgotten by most. The person who envisions the race must also envision the plan for the course. Without a plan—without written directions—they could run far off course and perhaps never finish the race at all.

Consequently, every race has a plan. A course is set with arrows, flags, and people along the way to point the runner in the right direction. The vision of the race course is clearly written for the runner.

Your vision, your purpose in God's plan, is very similar. The Lord has believers who will desire to run along side you and assist with the accomplishment of your vision. If there is no written course, direction, or plan for them to observe, it will be difficult for anyone, no matter how enthusiastic, to run with or proclaim your dream. You *must* write your vision down.

Multitudes of people are waiting anxiously for a dream to run with. Although God has given His people many such visions, only those who have written them down will enjoy the reward of others running with them.

As I meditated on this scripture in Habakkuk chapter two, the Holy Spirit revealed to me just how this principle operates. Speaking to me in His language, I saw a vision—a picture in my mind. In the picture, I saw a bright red fire truck adorned with chrome handles and huge ladders sitting motionless by the curbside of a city street. There were no firemen around it. People walked by and casually glanced at the gleaming machine, but no one stopped or seemed interested in the truck.

Then I saw a second fire engine. This truck was an exact duplicate of the first, but it came screaming down the narrow street with lights flashing and sirens blaring. People started leaping into their cars and chasing the speeding truck to its destination. Then the Lord spoke in my spirit and said through my thoughts, ''People don't follow parked fire trucks. They follow the truck that makes noise as it goes. When you get your vision written out and begin to proclaim it, people will follow you, too.'' That word changed my life. I hope it changes yours.

Once you have received a vision from the Lord and have written it down, you must share it with others. Remember, it is the moving fire truck—the one with an obvious purpose in mind—that people follow. It is also the fire truck that makes noise as it moves. You must let people know you have a vision and a purpose in life. God has people waiting to rally behind you to help you walk out and succeed with that vision, but you must give them opportunity to hear it.

When I launched Circus Alleluia Ministries, all I had to go on was one thought: start a circus to the glory of Jesus Christ. That was my total vision. If I had been content to allow my vision to remain a mere idea in my mind, Circus Alleluia would never have come to pass. But I took that thought and wrote it down. I began to write down every idea that could enlarge and advance that thought. Then I began sharing those ideas with others.

An entire year passed before the first runner joined me in the race. That runner was my wife, Meg. Soon a second runner, my mother, caught the vision. She was followed a few months later by my pastor. About three months after the pastor began running with us, the majority of our congregation was in hot pursuit. Today, thousands of people across the country believe in and run along side our vision. Why? Because we did not let the fire engines sit quietly by the curb. We hit the sirens, flashed the lights, and took off. Literally thousands of people have been affected by that one idea because I wrote it plainly and shared it with others.

Several years ago, as I was praying, the Lord promised, "If you will place the vision of Circus Alleluia Ministries in the hands of people, I will place it in their hearts. You must give Me something to work with so those who wish to run with your ministry will have opportunity." I heeded that promise, and it has proven true.

Anyone who has a vision or a ministry of any sort will require the assistance of others to assure its completion. Therefore, you must write out your vision. Make it something tangible and visible. Then place it in the hands of people. God will put it in their hearts, and they will run with you. You may hand out thousands of flyers with your vision on it and see only one person respond, but that one person may be all you need to get a major portion of your vision completed. The Bible says that the Lord is able to save by many or by few. (See 1 Samuel 14:6.) Don't be concerned about the number of runners in the race with you. Do as the

Lord commands. Write the vision plainly so those who read it may easily understand its course and destination.

How To Outline Your Vision

In the next chapter, I will go into great detail concerning the production of a precise written plan. However, at this point I would like to share the proper way to produce an outline form of your vision. This outline is what you should share with those you are attempting to enlist into the ranks of runners for your vision.

1. *Avoid constructing a long, wordy piece of literature.* An overview concise enough to fit on one piece of paper is all you need. Remember, when someone is running, it is hard to read a great deal of copy. Advertisers have known this for years; that is why most billboards possess large graphics and few words. If it works for Madison Avenue, it will work for you. Keep it short and to the point. Simplicity is the key.

2. *Divide your goals into past, present, and future categories.* Letting people know that you have already accomplished part of your vision, even if it is just preparing your plan, is impressive. It allows them to see that you are quite serious about your vision—an important point in gaining

faithful partners. Having a destination is great, but allowing others to see that you have already plotted a course is even more vital.

3. If possible, *a photo or some appropriate piece of artwork should adorn your publication.*

4. *Conclude your vision sheet with an open invitation for others to run with you.* This invitation may include a call for prayer, finances, or physical help. (See Figure 6-A.)

Writing our visions and dreams down is a must for success in achieving them. The Lord wants us to solidify and focus our purpose so those seeking direction themselves may see our vision and unite with us in the cause. Our purpose will actually become the purpose of others, a responsibility that rests in the proper display of that purpose.

Having placed your vision on paper, you will then be ready for the next important step—developing the plans for accomplishing the vision. Make no mistake about it. Your vision will require a great deal of planning. All too often this step is neglected. Such neglect is deadly to one's dream. Pour over the following chapter again and again until it becomes a part of you.

Remember, writing your vision is the first step in planning your vision. Without a written plan, your vision will remain silent and immobile—a vehicle of God's power doomed to a lonely death on the roadside of His perfect will.

THE VISION OF
CIRCUS ALLELUIA
BEGINNINGS

Bill Greenman is the Founder and Director of *Circus Alleluia*. While attending Florida State University, Bill became actively involved in the university's internationally famous Flying High Circus. Over the 3½ years he spent in Flying High, Bill learned a variety of acts, including slackwire, juggling, and flying trapeze. During this time, he married his lovely wife, Melanie, a trapeze and high wire artist in Flying High. Upon graduation, Bill and Melanie entered the professional circus world with aspirations of stardom. The Lord, however, had other plans. After a disappointing first season and a short engagement with a small traveling show, the Greenmans ended their circus careers and vowed never to perform again unless it was to the glory of Jesus Christ. The Lord honored their promise by giving Bill the vision for *Circus Alleluia*. Early in 1978, just twelve months after leaving the professional circus, Bill and Melanie began *Circus Alleluia* with a $25 donation they received for juggling at a youth retreat. Today that $25 has rapidly multiplied to build the only circus of its kind—*Circus Alleluia!*

SINCE THEN

•Thousands have been saved, healed, delivered, and baptized in the Holy Spirit through this ministry. In prisons, juvenile homes, schools, and civic auditoriums, the same miraculous results always occur. The Holy Spirit never fails to prove the reality of our risen Lord—Jesus Christ!

•*Circus Alleluia* has crisscrossed the eastern half of the United States many times, as well as into the provinces of Canada.

•The Christian Broadcasting Network (CBN) has produced a special presentation of this ministry for its international 700 Club broadcasts.

•Offers have come in from Africa, Central America, India, England, and coast-to-coast in the United States, including Alaska, to perform and minster!

Figure 6-A

THE FUTURE!

**Our goal: Use every available means to "say among the nations, 'Our God Reigns'" (Psalm 96:10).

Two fifteen-member circus troupes
One full-time, one part-time.

Sawdust
Our monthly teaching and newsletter, began in the fall of 1978 with one page; it is now four pages and growing.

College of Performing Arts
Teachers/Ministers with estabished skills in the arts to use those skills to preach the gospel.
Complete with on-the-job training in local ministry.
Beginning with video school and progressing to fully staffed college.

Audio-Visual Teachings
Slides, tapes, video, films that use the circus and other performing arts to teach biblical principles.
For use in schools, churches, and evangelistic outreaches.

TV Specials
On secular, prime-time television.
Broadcasting actual ministry performances of the circus and performing arts, complete with gospel invitation and signs, wonders, and healings as they happen.
Local phone banks and follow-up.

World Travel
Taking the circus to every country that will open to it.

CALL TO PRAYER

This vision shall be done! We want you to be a part of it. We ask you to lay your hands on this vision daily and pray in the spirit with thanksgiving. Believe with us now, for "All things are possible to him who believes!" (Mark 9:23). Amen!

Figure 6-B

7

PLANNING YOUR VISION

By utilizing the fundamentals of planning, you will discover that the success of your vision is almost guaranteed. I say almost because as with anything, *action* is the final step to realization. But before you can proceed with your dream, you must know exactly where it will take you and the route you will follow, as I mentioned in the previous chapter. Therefore, we will concentrate heavily on mapping out your step-by-step plan for transforming your vision from the invisible within you to the visible of your personal, daily, down-to-earth life.

Proverbs 21:5 cautions us, "The plans of the diligent lead surely to advantage, but everyone who is hasty comes surely to poverty." The Lord declares here that planning will give you a definite advantage. I believe this advantage will touch every area of your life. The advantage with people, money, time, and with the Lord Himself will be the fruit of a well-organized plan.

Wise planning demands diligence. Diligence dictates that no matter what obstacles may bar your way, you never cease in your quest. You always pick up where you were delayed and press forward again. A person with a plan before him finds the exercise of such diligence a simple task because no matter how many times he is side-tracked, he knows the course and can therefore easily resume his journey. For instance, you may have six goals in your plan and become sidetracked by other obligations during goal number four. By simply pulling out your vision plan and discovering where you got derailed, you can find your next goal. It will come clearly into view. The advantage of a good plan is obvious.

Let's take a look at the second part of Proverbs 21:5, which speaks of being hasty. Poverty and destruction await those in a frenzied rush to accomplish their visions. Most believers are so zealous to do God's will that they fail to plan and, instead, run aimlessly with no clear course for their actions. These people are so interested in reaching the finish line that they never find out how to get there.

If you want to succeed in your purpose, you must have a plan. Such planning will require a good deal of time to formulate. This expenditure of time is, again, a definite tip in favor of the planner in the cost versus benefit scale. Haste *does* make waste, and planning *does* bring advantage.

Proverbs 20:5 says, "A plan in the heart of a man is like deep water, but a man of understanding draws it out." As I stated in the fourth chapter, the initial thought of your vision is like a seed. Within that seed are all the plans you will ever need to produce the fruit of that vision. Every one of those plans is within you *right now* in the deep well of your heart. You must reach down into that well and draw those plans up. Proverbs 4:23 affirms that out of the heart come the issues of life. Remember, your vision is a source of life to you.

Meditation—The Key To Wise Planning

How do we draw forth those plans from within us? I believe that Psalm 1:2-3 presents the finest explanation:

> But his delight is in the law of the Lord, and in His law he meditates day and night. And he will be like a tree firmly planted by streams of water, which yields its fruit in its season, and its leaf does not wither; and whatever he does, he prospers.

Meditation is the key to wise planning. The Lord states here that the man who meditates on His Word will be like a tree growing at the water's edge. Such a tree draws its nutrients through its root system directly from the life-giving stream. Because it has a supply to draw from, the tree is capable of producing much fruit.

Producing the fruit of your vision is the ultimate goal of your life. Meditating on your vision, your purpose, and the Word of God will cause the necessary plans to come up within you. Just as water draws up through the root system and out the branches of a tree, meditation will cause those thoughts, ideas, goals, and plans to flow from your spirit up into your mind so you may write them down.

Meditation is merely thinking about, dwelling on, musing over, or discussing your vision. Quite simply, it is daydreaming.

In the initial weeks and months of my commitment to the vision of Circus Alleluia Ministries, I spent a great amount of time thinking and daydreaming about its creation and development. It was during these times of meditation that the Holy Spirit began to reveal to me the various aspects of the plan. Deep in my mind, I actually beheld pictures. I saw in my imagination how we would run our show and the proper technique for sharing our personal testimonies. I observed the rigging set-ups in their completed form, and I visualized myself delivering the invitation at the close of the performance. In my mind's eye, I saw the kind of vehicles we would drive and what follow-up materials we would need. It was all quite clear.

I have continued to use this picturesque method of reception through the years, and our ministry has borne much fruit because of it. This is not some eerie clairvoyant technique. It's simply allowing the Holy Spirit to paint His will on the canvas of my sanctified imagination. And it is done in an attitude of faith and prayer.

When you daydream about your vision, you will begin to draw goals and ideas from your spirit that have been placed there by the Lord. These goals and ideas will be segments of the plan for your vision. A word of caution here, however: To receive the proper plan while meditating on your particular purpose, you must confirm each goal the Lord discloses to you. It will take time for such confirmation, and it may even seem tedious. But, remember, as we read in Proverbs 21:5, those who are hasty will be destined for poverty. Don't be in a hurry to receive your plans or to walk them out. God's timing is perfect. You can trust Him.

Finally, when these thoughts, ideas, and plans come as you meditate and draw them from within you, write them down. Keep pencil and paper near you during times of meditation. You *must* write down these plans. You should never enter a time of communication with the Lord without a writing utensil handy. Do not rely on your memory. Rely on what God's Word says. The Bible orders us to write out the vision. I suggest that you purchase a notebook and entitle it, "Visions and Dreams," "Plans, Thoughts, and Ideas," or something along that line. When praying, keep that notebook with you so that when the Holy Spirit speaks those thoughts and ideas will not be lost.

Writing Down Your Goals

Wise planning requires clear cut goals. Every success-oriented publication I have ever read agrees on this one point. Your purpose will demand such precise goals, too. The best place to start is with a statement—one or two sentences—that clarifies the purpose of your vision or dream. For every vision and dream He gives His people, the Lord has a very specific purpose. This purpose will accomplish two different things: It will help people, and it will glorify God. Both of these items should somehow be included in your purpose statement.

The following example is from the purpose statement for Circus Alleluia Ministries: "Our purpose is to: 1) proclaim the gospel of Jesus Christ and administer its benefits worldwide, 2) disciple and train others to do as we have done. This will be accomplished through the use of every available printed and electronic media and all of the performing arts." This is a basic purpose statement, but it will give you a good idea where to start. Your purpose statement will allow those who wish to run with you to understand easily what you and your vision are all about.

Next you should list the major goals that will help you accomplish the purpose. For instance, in Circus Alleluia Ministries, we have six major goals:

1. Two circus troupes—one full-time, one part-time.

2. Publications—printing books, tracts, etc.

3. Audio/visual—producing tapes, films, videos.

4. Television specials of the Circus and other performing arts on secular stations.

5. World travel—taking the Circus to every nation.

6. A performing arts college to train those with established skills to utilize their abilities in proclaiming the gospel.

Such major goals, along with your purpose statement, should be written concisely. Once these have been fine-tuned, your vision will be ready to share with the runners who are helping you. A one-page publication is usually adequate to spread the information needed to enlist runners interested in your mission. (See Figure 6-B.)

Such production of one's personal vision may not be necessary in most believers' lives. Since my vision is a ministry, my particular purpose requires the support of a good deal more runners than someone with a vision of helps or nursery work. But regardless of the purpose entrusted to you by the Father, your creation of such an outline is still of infinite value. Even if you are the only person who ever reads the vision you pen, which is unlikely, it will allow you the benefit of a clearly focused set of guidelines by which to live your life. The ability to go back to that paper again and again to refresh your motivation is priceless. It becomes an anchor in the storm and a tower of truth when doubts bombard you.

These six goals of Circus Alleluia Ministries are the major steps we will take to attain our ultimate goal as proclaimed in our purpose statement. Within each of these major goals are packed many minor goals. For instance, one of our goals is to have two traveling circus troupes. To reach that goal, we must recruit new·performers, build or purchase new equipment, acquire more vehicles, and so on.

These minor goals consist of even smaller goals. In order to recruit performers, I must research the possible sources of potential acrobats and set up meetings with those I wish to interview. Minor and sub-minor goals are the stepping stones to achieving the major goals that will make it possible for you to fulfill your overall purpose.

In a race there are check points and sign posts to keep you pointed in the right direction. These let you know how far you have gone and how far you have to go. Your goals, both major and minor, are similar. As you accomplish each goal, you know exactly where you are in the overall vision, and you know how far you have to go.

Just like check points in a race, your major and minor goals must be set in a certain order. This order is called *prioritizing*. Some of your goals will take higher precedence than others. For instance, before I can put two circus troupes on the road, I must have proper personnel. Before I recruit the personnel, I must acquire the training facilities. It does me no good to have a Greyhound bus ready to roll across the country if there are no performers to place in that bus because we don't have any trapeze bars, juggling clubs, or trampolines on which to practice.

As you can see, certain goals come before others. This is known as placing your goals in correct priority.

An excellent way to prioritize your goals is to use a process called *backward planning* or *reverse planning*. Simply walk out your plan by beginning at the ultimate goal and work backward to your present location. First, write down each major goal on separate sheets of paper. Second, list all the necessary minor steps that must be realized to accomplish each major goal. Be sure to list each minor and sub-minor goal. (See Figure 7-A.) Once you have listed all the required steps, review them to make sure you haven't missed any points.

After your review is complete, list your goals in proper order, first to last, on a new sheet of paper. (See Figure 7-B.) With that accomplished, you now have a precision plan set before you with all the check points at hand. I suggest that you acquire a three-ring notebook, which can be divided into the major sections of your purpose. If there is any shift in priorities or major goals are subtracted or added along the way, their individual sheets of paper can be rearranged or removed accordingly. This type of planning is valuable for accomplishing any purpose, especially the purpose God has for your life.

Tapping Your Resources

Each goal that you have set will require certain resources to accomplish it. In his book, *Biblical Management,* author and businessman Myron Rush lists six headings under which every resource can be fitted. There may be one hundred items under each but only six headings. Using these headings, you can make a master resources list for anything you need to do. I employed this list while in charge of promotions for all special events at my home church. Once I became familiar with the system, I could sit down with this list and plan an entire two or three day seminar within ten minutes. Every detail of that seminar would be covered. I could know who, where, when, and how much it would take to accomplish any project. I now use this same master checklist for my own ministry, as well as for my personal endeavors. Such a list is a must for anyone stepping into the realm of planning for success.

The six main resources covered by the master planning checklist are as follows:

1. *People*

People are your most important resource. You must know your goals and decide what specific people are needed to accomplish those goals. When I planned a seminar for church, I needed artists, people for mail-outs, ushers, counselors, nursery workers, sound and video technicians, sales people, people to plan and cater luncheons, people to transport guest speakers, and, of course, custodians. I wrote down the name of every person who might possibly fit the need. Once done, I informed them of my need for their services.

2. *Facility*

Exactly what kind of facility will you need to accomplish your goal? When we planned our seminars, all we needed was our church building. There were, however, many parts of the church building that we would utilize. We knew we would need the nursery, print shop, restrooms, main sanctuary, pastor's lounge, overflow room, kitchen, lunchroom, and so on. Once you set your goal, deciding on the type of facility you need is an easy task.

3. *Equipment*

What kind of equipment will you need to accomplish your goals? For our seminars, we needed sound equipment, lighting, video, printing, folding machines, typewriters, cassette players, and vans to transport people. Knowing the goal gave us insight into the equipment we needed.

4. *Supplies*

Supplies are those perishable items necessary to reach your goal. For our seminars, these included paper, pens, notebooks, cassettes, diapers for the nursery, stationery for letters, envelopes, gasoline for vehicles, and breath mints for our speakers. Your goal dictates your supplies.

5. *Cost*

What will it cost to accomplish the goal? Until you have figured out and listed the other resources above, you really cannot know. When we held our seminars, we listed the cost for such things as art, mailing, rentals, luncheons, advertising, hotels, honorariums, miscellaneous items, vehicle maintenance, and custodial service. After calculating the entire cost of our resources list, item by item, the total budget for our meeting would be known. There was no guess work involved. It was all down before us in black and white.

6. *Time*

Time entails two areas—first, the setting of *target dates*. Target dates, or TD's, put all of your goals into a time frame. If you don't set a TD, you probably won't get it done. You must establish a timetable for every goal—major and minor—within your vision.

For our seminars, if I needed to send out a publication or publicity poster to different churches, I would first calculate the date I wanted the poster to arrive. I would then count back from that date to determine when I wanted it printed. I would then count even further to know when the art work was to be completed. Finally, I had to decide when I should contact the artist. When all was planned and targeted, it would look something like this:

Camera ready art completed by September 24.
Printing finished by September 28.
Posters mailed by October 5.
Posters received by October 8.

By starting at my finish line and working backward, I knew my starting line. I needed only to reverse the order, and then I would know my target dates for each point. When you have a major goal, set target dates for each item under the goal. Set realistic targets that can be achieved easily to avoid putting too much pressure on yourself or those assisting you. Remember Proverbs 21:5, "The hasty come surely to poverty." Good planning dispels haste.

The second consideration under the resource of time is *management*. Time management itself requires planning. It requires planning routine events in a certain time slot every day, every week, every month, and every year. When you know what needs to be done one month from now, you can plan your weeks, days, hours, and minutes throughout that month. I used to wander aimlessly through my days, bouncing from crisis to crisis, because I did not have my time scheduled. I was a poor manager of my time.

When I discovered that I could plan each day, hour by hour, even minute by minute, if necessary, I began to do so. I found I accomplished much more and was much happier, less anxious, and less pressured because I knew exactly what was supposed to happen and when. But I am not in bondage to time management. I avoid over-scheduling myself, which is all too easy to do. I allow myself time each day to handle unforeseen crises and emergencies. Consequently, I am accomplishing more in a shorter amount of time because my time is well-managed.

It has been said that if you inherited $88,000, you would surely spend some, save some, and invest some. If you expect to live ten more years, you will have 88,000 hours at your disposal. I suggest that you manage it well. The best way to begin is by purchasing a daily planning guide that has the hours of the day listed. Place routine items in certain hours, and do your best to accomplish those items during the scheduled time. Your time management can be as complicated or as simple as you wish. The choice is yours. I cannot over-emphasize the value of managing your time on a daily basis. It will not only relieve you of a great deal of unnecessary anxiety but will also assist you in the management of the target dates set for the goals in your vision.

Once you have developed a planning list of resources, you can begin to work toward any goal. As you progress toward the goal, you merely check off the items as they are accomplished. I suggest making a blank master list that you can copy and fill in for any project or goal. (See Figure 7-C.) Then all you need do each time is write the name of the goal at the top and fill in the blanks.

Planning's Final Step

Once all of your plans have been made and resources have been mapped out, you must commit the entire work to the Lord: "Commit your works to the Lord, and your plans will be established. . . . The mind of man plans his way, but the Lord directs his steps" (Proverbs 16:3,9).

This is obviously a simple task to agree to yet a frustrating one to comply with. How easily we can hang on to our dreams and plans. Our motives may be quite pure, desiring to perform the work at hand for the glory of our King. However, should the King require our hand to be applied elsewhere, our death grip may be hard to release.

In verse three, the word "commit" means "to roll upon, to place in God's hands." Rolling our works upon Him for His perfect timing can prove agonizing, to be sure. His directions can, at times, seem ridiculously wrong for our vision. But this promise from Proverbs is our security. Plans are written by us, but their establishment is His responsibility. Actually, that releases us from the fear of relying on our own finite understanding to make our vision happen. The word "work" spoken of in verse nine denotes the action taken to perform your plan. You must be willing to let His timing for the sequence of events take precedence over your own. When you commit your works to the Lord in such manner, He will see to it that your plans are fulfilled.

Your vision is a seed within you filled with all the plans necessary for full growth. You must draw those visions and dreams from your heart through meditating on your vision and on the Word of God itself. As these plans begin to flow from within you, you must apply them in practical ways.

Write down your purpose. List the goals that will help you accomplish that purpose. Arrange those goals in proper order, and uncover the resources necessary to accomplish them. Soon you will have the entire plan before you.

Finally, you must hand this plan—this vision— over to God for Him to orchestrate. But that is no time to sit back on your blessed assurance; for, in order to direct your plans, the Lord will need your assistance in supplying the necessary power.

Figure 7-A

Major Goal: *Publications*

I. Children's Book (Minor Goal)

    A. Send art and manuscript to publisher
    B. Proof finished manuscript
    C. Approve artwork finals
    D. Approve edited manuscript
    E. Approve artwork roughs
    F. Locate proofreaders or editor
        1. Edit copy of rough draft
        2. Proof for errors
    G. Give typed copy of rough draft to artist
    H. Locate artist
    I. Give tape to typist
        1. Dictaphone
    J. Dictate rough draft on audio tape
        1. Audio tape
        2. Recorder
    K. Write rough draft in notebook
    L. Outline story plot
    M. Develop characters for story
    N. Decide story idea to use
    O. List ten (10) story ideas
        1. Spiral notebook
        2. Pencil or pen
    P. Decide age group desired to reach

Figure 7-B

Major Goal: *Publications*

I. Children's Book (Minor Goal)
  A. Decide age group desired to reach
  B. List ten (10) story ideas
      1. Spiral notebook
      1. Pencil or pen
  C. Decide story idea to use
  D. Develop characters for story
  E. Outline story plot
  F. Write rough draft in notebook
  G. Dictate rough draft on audio tape
      1. Audio tape
      2. Recorder
  H. Give tape to typist
      1. Dictaphone
  I. Locate artist
  J. Give typed copy of rough draft to artist
  K. Locate proofreaders or editors
      1. Edit copy of rough draft
      2. Proof for errors
  L. Approve artwork roughs
  M. Approve edited manuscript
  N. Approve artwork finals
  O. Proof finished manuscript
  P. Send art and manuscript to the publisher

Figure 7-C

SEMINAR CHECKLIST

Facility	Personnel	Target Date	Cost
a. Sanctuary	_____	_____	_____
b. Portable B	_____	_____	_____
c. Nursery	_____	_____	_____
d. Print Shop	_____	_____	_____
e. Kitchen	_____	_____	_____

Equipment			
a. Risers	_____	_____	_____
b. Chairs	_____	_____	_____
c. Lights	_____	_____	_____
d. Video	_____	_____	_____
e. Water for Speaker	_____	_____	_____

People			
a. Ushers	_____	_____	_____
b. Hosts & Hostesses	_____	_____	_____
c. Cameraman	_____	_____	_____
d. Hospitality	_____	_____	_____
e. Artist	_____	_____	_____
f. Radio Announcer	_____	_____	_____
g. Printer	_____	_____	_____
h. Book Tables	_____	_____	_____
i. Janitor	_____	_____	_____

4. Supplies

a. Video Tapes _____ _____ _____
b. Audio
   Cassettes _____ _____ _____
c. Offering Env. _____ _____ _____
d. Paper
   (Mailouts) _____ _____ _____
e. Mailing List _____ _____ _____

5. Time
Schedule

a. Personnel con-
   tacted _____ _____ _____
b. Motel rooms
   reserved _____ _____ _____
c. Art work done _____ _____ _____
d. Printing done _____ _____ _____
e. Radio ads
   done _____ _____ _____
f. Radio ads
   sent _____ _____ _____
g. Mailouts
   mailed _____ _____ _____
h. Rentals placed _____ _____ _____
i. Rentals
   delivered _____ _____ _____
j. Newspaper ads
   placed _____ _____ _____

125

8

RELEASING THE POWER

Creating your dream will require a tremendous amount of power and energy. Such power is readily available to every believer in the Lord Jesus Christ. In fact, we all release this power on a daily basis, oftentimes unaware of having done so. When you, however, as a believer, knowingly release this creative power with faith and understanding to back it up, the full measure of Mark 9:23 will be yours: "All things are possible to him who believes."

Created In His Image

> Then God said, "Let Us make man in Our image, according to Our likeness; and let them rule over the fish of the sea and over the birds of the sky and over the cattle and over all the earth, and over every creeping thing that creeps on the earth"—Genesis 1:26.

This verse states that we are made in the exact likeness of Almighty God. We have the same basic features, the same mind, and the same characteristics (barring our sin nature, of course). Adam was the image of God. As sin-cleansed believers in Christ Jesus, so are we.

"Whoever believes that Jesus is the Christ is born of God; and whoever loves the Father loves the child born of Him" (1 John 5:1). We are children of God and therefore have His attributes, just as any earthly child has those of his father. My three children all have the same amount of limbs, eyes, ears, motor abilities, etc. that I possess. They even look a great deal like me in certain features—like their facial structure and body type. These physical traits that my children possess, because I am their father, are paralleled in the spiritual by the traits we possess because God is our Father.

Although the attributes of God (love, joy, peace, faith, and so on) belong to us, we will focus on one particular aspect of His person in this chapter—His creative power. The same creative power that produced our universe is available to you and me, as children made in the likeness and image of the Lord Almighty through Christ.

The Source Of Power

To discover this creative power, we need only observe our heavenly Father in the first chapter of the book of Genesis:

In the beginning God created the heavens and the earth. And the earth was formless and void, and darkness was over the surface of the deep; and the Spirit of God was moving over the surface of the waters.

Then God said, "Let there be light," and there was light. . . . Then God said, "Let there be an expanse in the midst of the waters, and let it separate the waters from the waters." And God made the expanse, and separated the waters which were below the expanse from the waters which were above the expanse; and it was so. . . .

Then God said, "Let the waters that are below the heavens be gathered into one place, and let dry land appear"; and it was so. . . . Then God said, "Let the earth sprout vegetation, plants yielding seed, and fruit trees bearing fruit after their kind, with seed in them, on the earth . . ." and it was so. . . .

Then God said, "Let there be lights in the expanse of the heavens to separate the day from the night, and let them be for signs, and for seasons, and for days and years; and let them be for lights in the expanse of the heavens to give light on the earth"; and it was so.

Then God said, "Let the waters teem with swarms of living creatures, and let birds fly above the earth in the open expanse of the heavens." And God created the great sea monsters, and every living creature that moves, with which the water swarmed after their kind, and every winged bird after its kind; and God saw that it was good. . . .

Then God said, "Let the earth bring forth living creatures after their kind; cattle and creeping things and beasts of the earth after their kind"; and it was so. . . . Then God said, "Let Us make man in Our image, according to Our likeness; and let them rule over the fish of the sea and over the birds of the sky and over the cattle and over all the earth, and over every creeping thing that creeps on the earth"—Genesis 1:1-26.

Now take a marking pen, reread these verses, and underline the words "God said" as you go. The Lord spoke eleven times, and eleven times His words became reality. Read Genesis 1:1 again. Notice the phrase, "God created." *How* did He create? He did so with His word. The following verses from the New Testament explain this fact quite well.

"By faith we understand that the worlds were prepared by the word of God, so that what is seen was not made out of things which are visible" (Hebrews 11:3). Until He spoke, nothing existed but God and the vision of what we now know as earth, animals, stars, and people. The Lord God took the invisible images of what He saw within His imagination and spoke words of life that actually catapulted those images into visible, real substance.

We, as God's children, made in His image and given His attributes, are capable of this same creative process. We will not create original substances such as light and earth, as He did, but we can cause that which God has already created to come into the realm of existence to fulfill His purpose for our life and the lives of others. We can actually speak our visions and dreams into reality. We can call into existence that which does not exist. Paul, commenting on the faith of Abraham in his letter to the Romans, clarifies this: "God, who gives life to the dead and calls into being that which does not exist" (Romans 4:17).

Faith From The Heart

As with all aspects of our Christian walk, this matter of creative power will require faith in God and His Word. As we read in Hebrews 11:3, even God Himself required this precious ingredient of faith to release His creative power. Mere conversation does not unleash His power. Only words backed by faith will realize its outpouring.

This fact is expressed beautifully by Jesus Him self in Mark 11:22-23:

> And Jesus answered, saying to them, "Have faith in God. Truly I say to you, whoever says to this mountain, 'Be taken up and cast into the sea,' and does not doubt in his heart, but believes that what he says is going to happen, it shall be granted him."

Notice that our faith is *in God,* not in ourselves. Never forget that. The creative power needed to see your God-given purpose take substance must be backed by God-centered faith. I am not speaking of positive mental attitude here but divine partnership and relationship with the Almighty. We are children putting absolute faith in our Father for His help to accomplish His will for our lives. The power we release to do so must be based on that faith and no other.

Such faith must emanate from our hearts. Our minds may reason and compute information, but we *believe* with our heart. And we will *always* speak what is most predominant in our heart. Even the hapless Pharisees were not exempt from the realities of this principle. Jesus made quite sure they understood it: "You brood of vipers, how can you, being evil, speak what is good? For the mouth speaks out of that which fills the heart" (Matthew 12:34).

This principle of heart belief is established unquestionably in Romans 10:10. In context, the apostle Paul is speaking of the correlation between believing and speaking. He factually states in this tenth verse that we believe with our hearts. To stop there, however, would make you unable to receive the benefits of what you believe. This verse illustrates the undeniable tag-team of faith in God, which is, *if you believe you will speak.*

Since this verse may leave us a bit vague in our understanding, the Lord explained it even more simply in 2 Corinthians 4:13: "But having the same spirit of faith, according to what is written, 'I believed, therefore I spoke,' we also believe, therefore also we speak."

Whatever you believe you will speak. This explains God's creative process. Everything He believed, He spoke. Everything He spoke, He said in faith. Words spoken in faith release the creative power of God.

A simple illustration can be found in the child playing with his beach bucket in the backyard sandbox. The little tyke methodically fills his toy with sand, packing it down firmly as he goes. When he is sure the little canister will hold not one grain more, he flips the bucket over with a thump to its top. After tapping the sides of the pot with a stick, he slowly lifts it from the floor of his imaginary seashore to reveal a perfect sand-castle, shaped exactly like the image inside his bucket.

The moral of this story is obvious. If you fill your bucket with sand, sand is all you get back—no matter how you disguise it. *Whatever you fill your heart with is what you will believe and what you will speak.*

When your heart is saturated with the vision and purpose God reveals for your life, your words will announce those contents. It is unavoidable. Your heart will pour forth words that speak of the vision in your heart. When it does, those words backed by faith and God's will for you will release their creative power to make that vision a reality. Like it or not, sweet fruit or sour, your Father's ability is yours. The joy is in knowing you can utilize that ability to His glory and for your life's fulfillment.

Filling The Heart

The key to power-packed speech is a heart overflowing with what you wish to create. Romans 10:17 explains, "So faith comes from hearing, and hearing by the word of Christ." Simply put, the more you hear, the more your heart contains of what you have heard. The more your heart contains, the greater the development of your faith toward what you are hearing. Through meditation on your vision, you fill your heart with its plan and fruit. Once full, your heart will pour forth words releasing the power to create what you have meditated upon.

Our hearts, as with the little boy's sand bucket, will hold exactly what we place in it and nothing else. We need only open up our hearts and pour out its contents with our words to see the contents become reality in our lives.

The Power Of Words

Words are dynamic and can actually dictate our future. They are so important that Jesus Himself has been appointed as High Priest over our words of faith. "Therefore, holy brethren, partakers of a heavenly calling, consider Jesus, the Apostle and High Priest of our confession" (Hebrews 3:1). If our Lord is that concerned about what we say, can we be any less watchful of our heart's contents?

Even those words we put no faith in are not to be taken lightly, for such idle words will also be accounted for: "And I say to you, that every careless word that men shall speak, they shall render account for it in the day of judgment" (Matthew 12:36). In fact, even our justification rides upon the creative wings of our own words: "For by your words you shall be justified, and by your words you shall be condemned" (Matthew 12:37).

Such truths may spark timidity or fear in some, but for those who know what their purpose is, the ability to release such power is thrilling. Taking our dreams and boldly proclaiming their creation is our responsibility and our right. We can give life to our vision or deal it a deathblow.

"Death and life are in the power of the tongue, and those who love it will eat its fruit" (Proverbs 18:21). The choice is ours. The power, accurately controlled by our believing heart, is released either way.

The key is speaking in faith, and this key rests heavily upon our ability to confirm what God has spoken. When you have followed the steps listed in chapter five and confirmed your vision, your capacity for faith in that vision will be enormously magnified. Doubt will find no room in your heart, and you will have no double-mindedness. When your vision has been confirmed, only faith will be evident within you. You will be free to open your heart to your vision and speak in faith when all your fears have been removed.

In the early planning stages of Circus Alleluia Ministries, I was the original Lone Ranger. I didn't even have a Tonto to reassure me with, "Ummm, that right, Kemosabe!"—not even my wife. (I had never given her a good reason to believe in any other dream, having blown everything I had tried up to that point). My mother, who usually defended me to some extent, was so convinced of my error with this Christian circus whim that she offered to pay my way to a prestigous seminary if I would forget the whole thing.

I was definitely a candidate for the doubt and unbelief academy, but doubt and unbelief never had a chance. I knew God had spoken, even though I did not know all of the confirmation points I have shared with you. Those I had learned, I used. I had God's purpose for me, and with that plan securely in my spirit, I began to fill my heart with its plans. I meditated and daydreamed about Circus Alleluia until I could not open my mouth without talking about it. It just rolled out of me.

Doubt, even in the face of being the lone believer, was never a question. Unbelief was history. My mouth spoke faith because my heart overflowed with the vision I had poured into it—God's vision for me. I believed it with my heart, and my heart spilled forth with words of confidence and power. Those words have since brought into existence what was once invisible.

We are made in the very image of Almighty God. His attributes are ours, and His creative thoughts and abilities are ours. Just as our Lord spoke all of creation into existence, from the invisible realm of His faith-filled heart, we, too, must do so with our own God-given dreams.

Words of life spoken from the abundance of your heart will manifest your purpose. Boldly proclaim your future. Release the creative power within you. But be certain that you do so from a heart filled with faith in the One who, with His own words, created all that exists. Then, having spoken, be ready to roll up your sleeves and get to work.

9

PUTTING FAITH INTO ACTION

Our entire Christian life should be one of action. We are never called to be passive observers waiting on the sidelines for our big brother, Jesus, to pick up the ball and run in the touchdown for us. *We* have been commissioned to go into all the world, make disciples of all nations, teach His commandments, cast out evil spirits, preach His Word, and lay hands on the sick. (See Matthew 28:18-20; Mark 16:15-18.)

If you are to see your God-given dream and purpose become a reality, you must understand from the beginning that no one else is going to make it happen. *You* are the deciding factor in the actual production of your vision. I am not saying that you will or must do *all* of the physical labor involved. On the contrary, the Lord will send runners to assist you in those matters.

What I am saying is that you cannot sit back on your righteous rocker and expect your visions to materialize out of thin air just because you know you have heard from the Lord. There is work involved. Achievement requires action. Muscle makes movement!

Work Your Plan

The old adage "Plan your work and work your plan" should be the watchword for anyone with a purpose for their life. In chapters six and seven we discussed several principles concerning the development of such a life plan. However, having a great plan with all your goals mapped out before you has little meaning to the Lord. Only those people that are *doing* something with their plans seem to catch His attention, as the following verses can attest.

> But prove yourselves *doers* of the word, and not merely hearers who delude themselves—James 1:22, *Italics added*.

> This book of the law shall not depart from your mouth, but you shall meditate on it day and night, so that you may be careful to *do* according to all that is written in it; for then you will *make* your way prosperous, and then you will have success—Joshua 1:8, *Italics added*.

And he shall be like a tree firmly planted by streams of water, which yields its fruit in its season, and its leaf does not wither, and in whatever he *does,* he prospers—Psalm 1:3, *Italics added*.

Poor is he who works with a negligent *hand,* but the hand of the diligent makes rich—Proverbs 10:4, *Italics added*.

As these scriptures state, God intends for His people to put what we believe into action. There are no shortcuts and no easy roads. Everyone who has ever received a directive from the Lord has had to act. Without action, success will be impossible. You and I are no exceptions.

Beware The Deceiver

I am a visionary person who views his purpose on grandiose scales reaping grandiose results. But impressive results come only from impressive efforts, not from mere visions. Consequently, for several years my ministry did not produce as it might have. My fulfillment came from the dreaming, planning, and initiating of the vision, but the follow-through held little delight for me. Not that I was lazy—I was just more content to go on to the next dream than to see the first one completed.

This proved to be the costly deception spoken of in James 1:22. I loved hearing God speak His vision to me, but I was not performing the work of it. I created my own deception, and it robbed me of the results God had intended. I meditated, filled my heart, and said what I believed, but fruit was minimal.

You see, confession of what you believe *is* necessary to release creative power. But without turning that power into action, your words hold little promise. A thousand repetitions of a scripture are no match for a single act of faith. James concluded his second chapter with that fact:

> What use is it, my brethren, if a man says he has faith, but he has no works? Can that faith save him? If a brother or sister is without clothing and in need of daily food, and one of you says to them, "Go in peace, be warmed and be filled," and yet you do not give them what is necessary for their body, what use is that? Even so faith, if it has no works, is dead, being by itself.
>
> But someone may well say, "You have faith, and I have works; show me your faith without the works, and I will show you my faith by my works." You believe that God is one. You do well; the demons also believe, and shudder. But are you willing to recognize, you

foolish fellow, that faith without works is useless? Was not Abraham our father justified by works, when he offered up Isaac his son on the altar? You see that faith was working with his works, and as a result of the works, faith was perfected; and the Scripture was fulfilled which says, "And Abraham believed God, and it was reckoned to him as righteousness," and he was called the friend of God. You see that a man is justified by works, and not by faith alone.

And in the same way was not Rahab the harlot also justified by works, when she received the messengers and sent them out by another way? For just as the body without the spirit is dead, so also faith without works is dead—James 1:14-26.

Faith merely spoken is lifeless. Faith teamed with action brings life.

After recognizing that the one responsible for the action aspect of my purpose in God's plan was *me,* I got to work immediately. I asked the Father to surround me with people who were more inclined to enjoy follow-through than dreaming. I needed runners, not more visionaries. Of course, the Lord complied. The outcome was increased achievement and, therefore, more time for me to dream and envision future plans. The deception was eliminated.

I suggest that you be thoroughly honest with yourself along this line. If you are more visionary than follow-through oriented, ask the Lord to give you the people necessary to complete the projects He gives you. *Action is no option*.

Lordship And Wisdom

I believe action is a very crucial point in the overall plan that God has for His people, both corporately and individually. Jesus Christ Himself taught that a wise man is one who obeys His commands and that action is the bottom line for anyone calling Him Lord. Luke 6:46-49 gives us this account of His exhortation on action:

> "And why do you call Me, 'Lord, Lord,' and do not do what I say? Everyone who comes to Me, and hears My words, and acts upon them, I will show you whom he is like: he is like a man building a house, who dug deep and laid a foundation upon the rock; and when a flood rose, the torrent burst against that house and could not shake it, because it had been well built. But the one who has heard, and has not acted

accordingly, is like a man who built a house upon the ground without any foundation; and the torrent burst against it and immediately it collapsed, and the ruin of the house was great."

The Lord is not impressed by our lip service or study habits. He wants action. When John the Baptist was confronted by the Pharisees' desire to be baptized, the prophet demanded, *"Bring forth fruit* in keeping with repentance; and do not suppose you can say to yourselves, 'We have Abraham as our father!' " (Matthew 3:8-9, *Italics added*). Our actions—our fruit—is the proof God seeks.

This doing of the word that God has given denotes both His written Word and the word or vision He gives us personally. Remember, John 10:27 asserted that we will *hear* His *voice,* not *read* His *Word.* The words we hear are just as much God's orders to us as His written Word. Our purpose, as revealed by the Holy Spirit, is His word to us. If we are truly to make Jesus our Lord, then we must *do* what He tells us (i.e., our vision).

Wise Up!

In verses 47-49 of Luke chapter six, Jesus proclaimed that acting upon the word of God is wisdom, having within it the ability to withstand the mighty storms of life. The reasoning behind this is simple. When we act on the word of God, we are establishing His Lordship in our lives. When Christ is your Lord, nothing can defeat you. "What then shall we say to these things? If God is for us, who is against us?" (Romans 8:31).

In my own vision, I have had numerous storms crash unmercifully against me. Several times I have felt that giving up would be much easier than pressing on. But every time those questioning thoughts flooded my brain, another voice rose up against them and said, "You are always caused to triumph in Christ Jesus! No weapon formed against you shall prosper! Greater is He that is in you than he that is in the world! You can do all things through Christ who strengthens you! Nothing shall be impossible for those who believe!" (See 2 Corinthians 2:14; Isaiah 54:17; 1 John 4:4; Philippians 4:13; Mark 9:23.)

That voice was the voice of the Holy Spirit encouraging me that my Lord is Christ and that none can stand against Him; therefore, none can defeat me. Because we had acted upon God's Word before the problems arose, each storm eventually blew by, and our ministry stood just as strong as ever. We could be bold in our confidence because we knew we had been obeying His commands. There was no scrambling to find the word of the Lord for our ministry and then attempting to pull it off before the flood washed us out. We performed His word when we received it.

The wise man built on the rock long before the storm ever slammed against his house. So it must be for us as we pursue our visions. We must constantly act on what the Lord speaks to us—but always in the confidence of His perfect timing.

Jesus said that some would call Him Lord who had not given Him evidence of Lordship. (See Luke 6:46.) Such evidence is the action we put to the word He gives us. Planning our work and working our plan is mandatory if we are truly to call Jesus our Lord. There can be no watching from the sidelines and no waiting for someone else to pick up our vision and run with it. Although many will assist us, it is inevitably up to us to act.

Take your vision, your dreams, and your plans, and put wheels to your faith. Step out and begin to do those things the Lord has instructed you to accomplish. Be a doer of His Word. Do not be deceived. Be sure that Jesus will be able to say to you, "Yes, I am your Lord."

10

HELPS HELP

The ministry of *helps* is perhaps the most misunderstood yet most widely needed ministry in the church world today. A powerfully anointed ministry gift, *helps* is listed along with apostles, prophets, teachers, miracles, gifts of healing, and diverse tongues.

> And God has appointed in the church, first apostles, second prophets, third teachers, then miracles, then gifts of healings, *helps,* administrations, various kinds of tongues—1 Corinthians 12:28, *Italics added.*

Helps is not a gift to be taken lightly but one that should be utilized by anyone with a designated vision and purpose for his life.

Remember the runners spoken of in Habakkuk 2:2? Runners are those who operate in the ministry of helps to assist you with your vision. You need the ministry of helps. You need to operate in it yourself, and you need others to operate in it to assist you. Remember, any vision that God imparts to you will invariably be too big for you to handle alone. Lone Ranger Christianity is *not* God's idea of quality ministry. He will ensure your need of others to help you. You *will* need runners.

This brings us to the most important principle in this book—that of sowing helps so you may reap helps. In 2 Corinthians 9:6 we are told, "Now this I say, he who sows sparingly shall also reap sparingly; and he who sows bountifully shall also reap bountifully." Whatever we sow we will reap. My suggestion to you is that you sow the ministry of helps bountifully into the lives of others who need assistance with *their* purpose and vision. By sowing bountifully, you will have a bountiful harvest coming to you when your vision expands to the point where you require more laborers.

Let me give you an example from my own life and ministry. In 1978, the vision for Circus Alleluia Ministries was a fire building in my heart. At the Lord's direction, my wife and I had moved to Tampa, Florida, and begun to attend Calvary Temple International Christian Center in the Northeast section of town. The pastor was and still is Dale Brooks. I shared my vision with Dale, and immediately he felt a witness in his spirit that it was from God. When he urged us to make Circus Alleluia a part of the ministry of Calvary Temple, we followed his advice.

Almost immediately, the Lord placed within my heart the desire to sow a major portion of my time and energy not into my circus ministry but into Dale's vision for his church. I had experienced firsthand the realities of God's sowing and reaping principles. Some years before, Meg and I had employed its laws to climb out of debt after quitting the professional circus world. I knew that it would work in this ministry of helps and that there would come a time in my ministry when I would be forced to enlist the support of many people. So I determined in my heart to obey this leading and sow the majority of my time and energy into my new pastor's vision.

I made myself available for whatever task was needed. At that time there were approximately twenty-five people attending the church services, so volunteer help was at a premium. I cleaned the bathrooms, vacuumed the church, scrubbed the baptistry, and mowed the acreage. My wife joined me in these times of sowing, not just for a couple of weeks but for the first several years of our own ministry. We taught the youth group, ran the print shop, sang in the choir, and took cars to the shop. If it needed to be done, we did it.

Meg and I also looked for other major ministries into which we could sow our time and energies. Whenever a large convention came to town, I volunteered my services as usher or counselor. I did this as an act of faith to sow seeds of help into these quality ministries. I sowed quality seed and gave them my best—the best of my abilities, the best of my time, and, of course, the best of my finances—because I wanted the best to come back to me.

Proverbs 6:6-11 speaks of an industrious little ant. The creature works hard through the summer to assure a sufficient food supply during the winter months. This illustrates my need to sow the ministry of helps during the time my own need was minimal. When my vision did increase, I could reap the necessary harvest. That is exactly what happened. After several years of sowing the seeds of faith into my pastor's vision and the visions of other men and women of God, I began to see a mighty harvest returning to me.

Today I am amazed at the ministry of helps I receive from those within my ministry. Their servant attitudes and willingness to help with the vision God has given me is at times intimidating. Their dedication to the vision of Circus Alleluia Ministries leaves me astounded. People from our church volunteer to work on our mailing lists, help with writing and typing, create the artwork, make the sparkling show costumes, and even build our equipment—mostly without us asking for their assistance. One day I asked God why He was blessing me so wonderfully with these selfless people. He immediately reminded me of all the years I had spent sowing my time and efforts into other ministries. I was merely reaping what I had sown.

Whatever your vision may be, you should sow quality time as a minister of helps into someone else's vision. In fact, I believe the majority of you will have a *vision* of a ministry of helps. Leaders are to direct the multitudes and will require the strength of those members to do so. If yours is a ministry of helps, what an exciting vision God has given you—to hold up the arms of a Moses or go before a Prophet of God to secure a place for a Last Supper.

The ministry of helps is scattered across the pages of the Old and New Testaments. Even Jesus Himself operated in the ministry of helps when He fed the five thousand and healed the multitudes. He was helping and assisting them. In fact, I do not believe God will give anyone a vision who is not involved in some way with the ministry of helps. Remember, any vision from God will always do two things: *one,* glorify God, and *two,* help people. Visions of mere survival are not in God's plan for His Church.

You will need people operating in the ministry of helps to further your vision from God. Therefore, before your need becomes too great, reach out and sow your time and effort as a minister of helps into someone else's vision. When you need it, your help will be there.

(I suggest that you read *The Ministry of Helps,* by Buddy Bell, a Harrison House publication. His practical application of this ministry is excellent.)

11

JACOB'S EXAMPLE

In this chapter, I would like to share with you a biblical example of a personal vision and its planning, implementation, and eventual rewards. This is the story of Jacob and his quest for freedom from the hand of his uncle, Laban.

In this story, we will see Jacob's need for a vision and how he found it and applied the writing of the vision. We will discover how he developed a plan and set goals, found his resources, obtained helps, and finally put them all in order on the way to seeing his vision accomplished. I believe that if you read this chapter again and again, comprehending this example with your heart, it will aid you in every vision and dream you receive from the Lord.

Jacob truly needed a vision. After faithfully serving Laban, his uncle, for twenty years, he had received little in return. Having taken two of Laban's daughters to be his wives, he had fathered many children. But financially and materially

Jacob was still in poverty. He longed to raise his family on his own land and not be under the dominion of his uncle.

The Lord was not ignorant of Jacob's plight. Therefore, God, through a vision, brought Jacob the solution to his problem. He shared with Jacob the avenue by which he could fulfill his desire for freedom. Jacob took hold of that vision, began to practice the principles we have discussed in this book, and successfully accomplished his goal on his own terms.

In Genesis 31:7-13, Jacob explains to Laban's sons just how he was able to acquire his freedom from their father:

> "Yet your father has cheated me and changed my wages ten times; however, God did not allow him to hurt me. If he spoke thus, 'The speckled shall be your wages,' then all the flock brought forth speckled; and if he spoke thus, 'The striped shall be your wages,' then all the flock brought forth striped. Thus God has taken away your father's livestock and given them to me.
>
> "And it came about at the time when the flock were mating that I lifted up my eyes and saw in a dream, and behold, the male goats which were mating were striped, speckled, and mottled. Then the angel of God said to me in the dream,

'Jacob,' and I said, 'Here I am.' And He said, 'Lift up, now, your eyes and see that all the male goats which are mating are striped, speckled, and mottled; for I have seen all that Laban has been doing to you. I am the God of Bethel, where you anointed a pillar, where you made a vow to Me; now arise, leave this land, and return to the land of your birth.' "

In verse eleven, the angel of the Lord speaks to Jacob and shows him a vision. In that vision, he sees the cattle of Laban mating. The angel says, "See that all the male goats . . . are striped, speckled, and mottled; for I have seen all that Laban has been doing to you."

God is giving precise instruction to Jacob. He is declaring, "Jacob, this is what *I* see. I see *all* those animals as spotted and speckled, and I want *you* to see them all as spotted and speckled, too." It is the solution to Jacob's dilemma. God is informing him through the language of the Holy Spirit, "Here is your way out. Here is the vision and dream you can build upon and formulate a plan with—one you can write down and run with. This is the way I will deliver you from the hand of Laban so you can see your vision and dream— your purpose in life—fulfilled!" Finally, in verse thirteen, the Lord urges Jacob to rise, leave the land of Laban, and go back to the land of his own family.

Now Jacob has a clear word from God. He knows that God wants him to leave Laban and step out on his own. He also has a plan for accomplishing that word. Jacob heeds these instructions and proceeds toward his ultimate goal, which is leaving Laban.

Jacob begins to formulate a plan. In Genesis 30:25-43, we see that plan unfold perfectly. Jacob tells Laban that he wishes to leave and take his family with him. Laban, understanding that Jacob is the real reason for his prosperity, pleads, "No, no stay! Name your price. Name your wages, and I'll give them to you."

On that offer, Jacob initiates his plan. He insists of Laban, "My wages are these: isolate all the spotted and speckled from all the pure colored cattle. Separate them three days distance, and give me care of all the pure colored cattle. Let your sons care for the spotted and speckled. Any spotted and speckled born to the pure colors in my care will be my wages." Of course, Laban thinks Jacob has presented a foolish offer and readily agrees to the terms. He knows that the chances of the pure color cattle birthing any substantial number of spotted and speckled offspring are minimal.

Jacob proceeds with his plan. His next major goal is that his pure colors begin to produce spotted and speckled animals. To accomplish this, he begins to write his vision and put it before those who will run with it—in this case, the pure colored cattle.

Jacob goes to the forest, cuts down many small trees, and chips away the bark so the trees and tree limbs will look spotted, speckled, and striped. He then places those trees and limbs before the cattle at the watering troughs. When the animals come to drink, they begin to mate.

The Fruit Of Diligence

Jacob's goal was to have all the animals conceive with the spotted and speckled rods right before them. Since he wanted to make sure that those which would produce his goal and vision were seeing what he saw, he placed his vision before the runners. When it came time to conceive and produce, Jacob made certain his vision was all they could see. And, of course, that is exactly what happened. The pure colored cattle began to produce spotted and speckled offspring!

After these mottle-colored animals were born, Jacob separated them to assure that none of the pure colors would mate with the streaked and spotted cattle. But he also made sure that the pure colored animals could see the spotted and speckled ones. Jacob did everything he could to keep his vision of spotted and speckled offspring before the pure colored flock. This would further that vision.

Jacob also gave special attention to those animals that seemed stronger and healthier. When they began to mate, he put the spotted rods directly in front of them, knowing that they would produce stronger, healthier spotted and speckled calves. But if he saw weak animals mating, he pulled the rods from before them so they would produce weaker, pure colored offspring that would be Laban's instead of his.

Jacob, having planned his work and worked his plan, was able to accomplish his major and minor goals and finally reach his ultimate vision of leaving his uncle's dominance.

But don't miss the time element here. Those animals did not bear offspring overnight. Many months and years passed during the working of Jacob's plan. Throughout the agonizingly slow months of the cattle's pregnancy, Jacob operated by faith that God's word to him was true. He had to keep pulling up and driving down those rods week after week before he saw any fruit. Visions and dreams, no matter how well planned, will take time to bear fruit. Jacob was obviously very patient and diligent. We, too, must follow that aspect of his example.

Let me briefly outline to you Jacob's tremendous illustration of finding, planning, developing resources, doing, and receiving the results of a personal vision.

1. Jacob had a vision, which was to leave Laban.
2. His purpose was to have a place of his own to raise his family.

3. His major goal was to acquire the abundance necessary to meet his vision.

4. The resources available to him were the flocks of Laban that he had been shepherding for twenty years. His goal was to acquire, as his wages, all of the spotted and speckled animals.

5. A minor goal was to separate the pure colors from the spotted and speckled.

6. Another sub-goal was to take the pure colors and make them produce spotted and speckled.

7. He wrote his vision in the branches and trees by carving spots and speckles in the bark.

8. He placed his vision before those who would run with it (which were the cattle).

9. He made it a point to give special attention to the strongest producers.

10. Over a period of several years, each goal was met, and his vision came to pass.

As we can see by this beautiful example, God is able to use anything to make your visions come to pass. When you have a word from the Lord, it is up to you to draw the plans.

It will also be up to you to walk out those plans. If God could use animals and tree limbs to further Jacob's purpose and vision, He can surely supply your needs on the way to fulfilling your dreams. This exciting account of Jacob in Genesis is an extraordinary example of receiving a vision from God and fulfilling it. But just as Jacob developed his plan, used his resources wisely, and eventually achieved his goal, you, too, can do the same.

12

DARE TO DREAM WITH GOD

I am truly excited for you as you approach the conclusion of this book. I know the Lord has begun to inspire you and enlarge your thinking so that you will dare to dream with Him. If you will dare to dream with God, then nothing will be impossible for you. Nothing is more exciting than dreaming God's dreams, and nothing is more fulfilling than accomplishing His vision for your life.

In this chapter, I want to share ten points—stepping stones—that you will probably experience during your time of developing and producing your purpose. As you read over these steps, I pray you will find encouragement and strength from them and will not give in to the discouragement that comes with the walking out of any dream from God.

You *will* be opposed. We are in a war with an enemy who will stop at nothing to obstruct the visions and purposes God has given His people.

If you know the steps beforehand, you can avoid many of the battles and many of the pitfalls that the enemy may set before you. Dare to dream. Dare to dream with God.

The Ten D's

1. *Delight*

The first step you must take as you dream with God is to delight yourself in the Lord: "*Delight* yourself in the Lord; and He will give you the desires of your heart" (Psalm 37:4). It should give you great joy and pleasure to spend time with the Lord—fellowshipping with Him through prayer, reading His Word, and worshipping Him. If your life is not filled with such pleasant times spent with the Lord, then dreaming His dreams will be difficult. Delighting yourself in the Lord is a prerequisite to opening your spirit to the things of God.

2. *Desire*

The second half of Psalm 37:4 explains that God will give us the desires of our heart. Once we begin to delight ourselves in the law of the Lord, He will personally give us the desires of our heart.

The word "desire" means to long for, to crave, or to covet. God will do two things with a desire. First, He will place the desires within our heart.

Second, He will cause those desires to become a reality in our lives. This is beautifully stated in Philippians 2:13: "For it is God who is at work in you, both to will and to work for His good pleasure."

In this verse we see that God will give us the *will,* the *want to,* and also the *ability* to perform His good pleasure. Obviously, any desire or dream God places in your heart will be within the realm of His good pleasure. The Lord will always confirm the desires He places within you. Such desires of the heart are always both life changing and life directing.

Ever since I can remember, I have had the desire to be a performer. It began in kindergarten when I stepped onto a stage for the first time in a Christmas play. Even that far back, I can remember thinking, "This is what I want to do. I like it here. I want to be here." I worked on the stage every year after that until I went to junior high. Then I began to use sports as my stage for several years, becoming involved in school athletics. I have always been a performer and have always loved entertaining people.

As children, my brothers and sisters and I often put on plays for neighborhood friends in our garage. I remember spending countless hours watching Hollywood musicals and dreaming of being a dancer, singer, or actor. It became a strong desire in my heart—something that I craved, longed for, and coveted. Finally, in my sophomore year at Florida State University, I stepped into the center ring of a circus tent and have been there ever since.

But before that happened, I had stepped onto a greater stage, one that was to direct my life even more than the circus. That was the stage of Christianity. I gave my heart to the Lord Jesus Christ in my freshman year of college, and my desires immediately changed. Oh, I still wished to be a performer, but now there was a new desire within me—a desire that vied for the place in my heart that performing had always held. That desire was to evangelize, win souls for Jesus Christ, and tell others how He could change their lives as He had changed mine. Unfortunately, it was five long years before that desire won out over the desire to perform.

The Lord has allowed me to fulfill both desires because both of them were given to me by His inspiration. He did not take my performing desire away when I finally gave Him complete control of my life's affairs. Instead, God graciously enhanced it by coupling it with my desire to win souls. Now, through the stages of circus, singing, teaching, and preaching, I am able to fulfill the two greatest desires of my heart.

It all started the moment I began to delight myself in the Lord completely—the moment I said, "You, Jesus, are my reason for living, not me anymore; and not my desire to be a star. But *You* are now the star. You are my reason to live. You are the Lord of my life!'' When I delighted myself in the Lord, He gave me the desires of my heart—greatly multiplied.

3. *Dream*

Proverbs 29:18 tells us, ''Where there is no vision, the people are unrestrained [unguided].'' People with no dream have no direction. When you begin to delight yourself in the Lord and He gives you the desires of your heart, those desires will come together in the form of a dream. He will take your desires and put them inside a dream (a vision) and then place that dream within your heart.

Webster's dictionary explains that a dream is ''a fond hope or a vision'' (the very vision we have discussed throughout this book). But how can you tell if your dreams or visions are from the Lord? As I have previously stated, Godly dreams will always accomplish two things. First, they will glorify God; and, second, they will help people. If the dream within your heart does not do these two things, it is not God's dream for you.

My desire was always to be a professional performer. I attained that dream without God. When I finally reached that goal, I realized it was not God's plan for me because He gained no glory from what I was doing. No one was being helped, uplifted, or exhorted to do great things for Him—not even me. It was merely a self-honoring dream.

When I placed the Lord on the throne of my life, He turned that dream into His dream. Now it glorifies the Lord and helps people all around the world.

4. *Destiny*

Once God has given you a dream, it will become your destiny. It will become your future. Proverbs 29:18 tells us that without a vision a person is "unrestrained." The opposite is true for those who have a vision. You will become restrained and guided. Your dream will guide you. Websters defines "destiny" as "an inevitable series of events or that which determines those events, that is, a supernatural thing." Webster is referring to God Himself, the supernatural entity who causes your destiny to occur.

If God's dream is your destiny, then He, of course, will be in on it. Your vision and purpose for your life will direct every step you take. It will become your future. When you have a dream, you must begin to plan that dream. As you plan that dream, you are planning your future and your destiny.

I made plans about the dream that was in my heart. I wanted Circus Alleluia to travel and win souls. Part of my vision was to hold seminars to teach others how to win souls. I desired to write papers and books, teach, and share with others what God was doing through our ministry.

I wanted to use every available means to spread the gospel. As I began to formulate the plan, I was formulating my future, which I have been living since 1977. (And I will most probably be living it when Jesus returns.) Your dream, like mine, will become your destiny.

5. *Decision*

Once God reveals your dream and you understand it as your destiny, a decision will confront you. You can decide "yes" you will follow the dream or "no" you will not.

Deuteronomy 30:19 explains that God has given us the choice of "life and death, the blessing and the curse." A vision always brings life because it brings purpose and guidance. When you choose to follow the dream that the Lord places in your heart, you will be choosing life. You will be choosing physical life, mental life, spiritual life, and emotional life because God's dream will encompass every area of your being.

If you choose not to live out the purpose God set for your life on earth, you will never find the peace you seek. You will have no success and no life.

Making such a decision is not a quick mental process. It will be a decision of the heart, and it will be a decision for life. Taking the necessary time to understand fully the cost of such a decision is not an option to you.

6. *Determination*

Having made the decision to run with the dream and vision that God placed in your heart, you will then be forced to exercise determination. Determination means a firm intention and a resolute purpose.

In Daniel 1:8, we see that the prophet, Daniel, possessed such a firm, resolute attitude. He determined not to eat from the table of the king who had captured him and his people. Daniel was a Jew and did not wish to eat food that had been sacrificed to idols by this heathen king. He would not defile his body, for he had given himself completely to God. Daniel was resolute, and nothing would change his mind. He was so firm in his purpose that he was willing to give his life for it.

When you decide to run with the dream God has placed in your spirit, you must determine that nothing will stop you. It is *after* you make the decision to go with the dreams of God that battles will begin. You wrestle an adversary who knows exactly what you are doing. The devil does not only live in this world but also in the world of the spirit. He knows the spiritual activity that surrounds you, for he can see the angels that go to and fro in your life.

Even as you read this, there are demonic forces that would try to make you discard what you have read. They will tell you, "No, this isn't for you. God really doesn't have a plan for your life. You re not supposed to be anything more than what ou are right now. Relax! What are you getting so xcited about?"

Do not listen to these satanic whisperings. You nust be determined that absolutely *nothing* will top you from carrying out what the Lord has alled you to do.

When I began Circus Alleluia Ministries, I made hat determined decision. I began to tell people bout my vision, and their reactions were anything ut positive. For the first nine months, no one vanted to be bothered with my dream. But I had letermined in my heart that I would attain the lream God had given me. I made the decision that f no one else ever believed in Circus Alleluia Ministries but me, I would still do everything ossible to make it happen.

Even now my determination is just as strong. f everyone left our ministry today, Circus Alleluia Ministries would not die because it is alive in me. Circus Alleluia is God's vision for me. That vision as consumed me, and I am determined that noth-ng will stop it from happening, except the Lord Himself.

When you dare to dream with God and make he decision to fulfill that dream, *you* will have o determine in your heart to live it no matter who grees or disagrees with you. Because of my nitial determination, thousands of others are now ust as determined to see Circus Alleluia Ministries ulfill its vision.

7. *Dedication*

After you have determined in your heart that you will act on the vision God has given you, you must dedicate yourself to it. Dedication means to devote to a sacred purpose or to set apart for the worship of Deity. Your dream will become sacred to you. Why? Because it is God's. Is God sacred to you? Of course He is! That means the dreams and visions He gives you will also be sacred.

The vision God has given me is sacred to me, and it has become my worship back to God. It is my worship to Deity. It is my life's work. I worship and praise God with whatever is produced through this ministry. If I were living out this dream only for myself, I would have stopped long ago because I don't think I am worth that much work. But God *is* worth it!

When you dedicate yourself, totally, to your dream, it will become a worship unto the Lord. It will become your praise, your devotion, and your sacred purpose. In Matthew 6:21, we are told by Jesus Himself, "Where your treasure is, there will your heart be also." The dream that God gives you will come from your heart. It will become your treasure and your sacred purpose.

8. *Discipline*

Once you have dedicated yourself, you must then exercise discipline. It will take discipline to

172

devote yourself to your dream. Discipline is the training that develops self-control, character, orderliness, and efficiency. In 1 Timothy 4:7, Paul explains that Timothy should discipline himself for the purpose of godliness. You must gain self-control and train yourself to be orderly and efficient in all you do.

I once heard a preacher say, "When I want to find out how godly a person is, I don't check their church attendance records—I go to their house and open up a closet!"

When I heard that, I went home and cleaned my closets. I hung up my clothes, put my shoes in order, and sorted and folded the clothes in my bureau drawers. That was the beginning of a discipline.

If you don't discipline yourself in everyday things, you won't discipline yourself when it comes to your ministry or your vision. How can God trust you with a world-reaching vision for your life if He can't even trust you to reach into your closet and hang up your clothes? You may be asking, "Does God really care about how tidy my bedroom is?" Absolutely! He said that if we will be faithful in little, He will put us in charge of much. (See Matthew 25:23; Luke 19:17.) It takes great discipline to be faithful in little things.

Discipline will require sacrifice, and it won't always be fun. Many times it won't be fun at all. But the more disciplined your life becomes, especially concerning your visions and dreams, the more you will accomplish for the Lord and the more peace and temperance you will have in your life.

I am a very social person and love to be around people. In my early years of ministry, God had to teach me to discipline myself. There were days when He told me, "I want you to go into your room and study My Word today." I would obey. Then friends would drop in. As I rose to greet them, the Lord would say, "Stay here and study."

Now these people were my friends, they were in my house, and they wanted to see me; but I would not get up. Once a close friend came to the bedroom door and said, "Hi, B.G.," but I didn't even speak to him because God was teaching me to be disciplined. He had said, "You spend this time with Me and discipline yourself to concentrate on Me and My Word." That may sound hard, but I needed it that way.

Those early years of discipline have more than paid for themselves. I have no regrets about the days that I locked myself in my bedroom to fellowship with God through His Word. Now I enjoy and look forward to such times. Yes, discipline requires sacrifice, but the rewards are always more than worth it.

9. *Diligence*

Discipline requires diligence. When you begin to discipline yourself by setting schedules and making plans to do certain things at certain times, you may not always accomplish what you planned to do. You may sleep late one morning when you meant to be up praying. You may be forced to go somewhere or do something at the time you set aside to study the Word. Or someone may invite you to dinner when you had planned to go jogging. Inevitably, circumstances will keep you from doing what you had planned to do. This is where diligence comes into play.

A disciplined man must be a diligent man. Diligence means to be constant, to make careful and continual effort. It means that you don't quit just because your schedule was derailed. You pick up where you left off and start again. The Bible states, "A righteous man falls seven times, and rises again" (Proverbs 24:16). That is diligence. Don't stop just because things go wrong for a day or two. Things may not go right for a couple of years! Just because your vision doesn't seem to be going according to your timing is no reason to quit.

I have often wondered in the last several years if my ministry would ever get off the ground. We have fought through difficult financial problems, sicknesses, injuries, and vital people suddenly leaving the ministry. At times I have wanted to throw in the towel. Sometimes I have even yelled at God and wanted to know why we had to go through these problems.

But I had made a decision to be diligent, and I would not quit. Nothing would make me stop.

175

No matter how hard I was knocked down, I would always get back up. Yes, we have had many trials, and I believe we have come out victorious in every one because we never gave up.

Quitters never win, and winners never quit. You will have to be diligent in your discipline. Romans 12:11 tells us not to lag behind in diligence but to be fervent in our spirit serving God. The Lord didn't say not to lag behind. He said we should not lag behind *in our diligence*. Rise up and pursue your dream again.

10. *Death*

At some time in your vision, maybe several times, death will come. You will do your best. You will be diligent, disciplined, determined, and devoted, but death will come. You cannot avoid it. *There will come a point in your dream when it must die.*

It is a godly principle. Jesus said it Himself: "Unless a grain of wheat falls into the earth and dies, it remains by itself alone; but if it dies, it bears much fruit" (John 12:24). You can see this principle time and again throughout the Bible.

Perhaps the greatest example of this principle is Christ Himself. Jesus spent three years in victory. There was hope for the world to be saved. He was the Messiah, God in the form of a man walking on the earth with us. God's vision of restoring Israel to rule over the world appeared to be at hand. Then tragedy struck, and the vision seemed to die. Jesus was executed and buried. It seemed that the entire dream and vision had been destroyed.

In reality, the principle of the seed—its seeming death and then resurrection—was in operation. After Jesus rose from the dead, God's vision was able to spread to every continent. It will eventually touch every nation in the world. As His fruit, we are able to bear more fruit—much more fruit than He could have borne by Himself.

At some point your dream and vision will die. God has a reason for this. Your vision must never become more important to you than He is. Many times, when we begin to embark on the vision God has for our lives, we develop tunnel-vision, seeing only that vision and nothing else. We become so locked into making that vision happen that it becomes the focal point of our lives. There is always the danger of your vision becoming more important to you than God.

In my own life, my vision of Circus Alleluia Ministries was forced to die for that very reason. A few years ago, my pastor came into my office and told me that the Lord shared with him that I was to become assistant pastor of our church. Immediately, I said, "I don't believe that was God." My desire was to be anything but a pastor. However, I had made the decision many years before that I would always pray over a word given to me by a spiritual man or woman.

So I prayed, and, amazingly, the Lord confirmed to me that I was indeed to become the assistant pastor. At that point my vision died.

My vision needed to die, for I had become hard in my heart toward the brethren in my church. I had grown tired of them coming to me with the same problems over and over again. I had grown tired of people telling me that the Word of God didn't work. I was just tired of people! My pat answer to everything was "Just do what the Word says" because I did not want to spend time counseling them.

I needed to become assistant pastor to soften my heart and rebuild and rekindle the flame of compassion within me. If I had gone on the road full-time in the circus ministry with that kind of attitude, I never would have lasted.

When I finally told my pastor that the Lord had confirmed to me to be assistant pastor, he looked me right in the eye and said, "I'm sorry, Bill, because I realize this means your vision must die." Three long years passed before I understood what those words meant. In fact, it was only days before I resigned as assistant pastor and stepped full-time into directing Circus Alleluia Ministries that I realized it. My vision did die during those years as I poured my time and efforts into the church.

Actually, the dream did not die completely. It just did not progress. It stayed in an almost dormant stage. We still performed, and many people were saved. There were still miracles, and we still produced our teaching papers. But there was no growth in the ministry. Because I did not understand the principles of death of a vision, I tried everything to make things happen for Circus Alleluia Ministries (C.A.M.). But all my efforts fell short because God was not in them.

Finally, those few days before my short career as assistant pastor ended, the Lord was able to share with me His reasons for C.A.M.'s "burial." He explained, "I had you put Circus on the shelf so that the seed of My compassion could take root and flow through you again. Your attitude that everyone should just get out of your way so you could get on with your vision had to be destroyed." He was right.

Those years as assistant pastor were not pleasant for me because of the death that occurred within me. However, I praise God for every moment of that time because it caused His compassion—His real love and concern for people—to be birthed within me. Now my heart breaks to see people hurting, no matter how many times they have been through the same problem. Now I long to reach out to people and help them.

You will not be able to avoid this tenth point— the apparent death of your vision. God will always test you. He will always search deep in your heart to determine if your vision is more important than His perfect will. I pray that you will allow the seed to fall into the ground and die. The resurrection to life that God will give it is far more valuable than its short time in the ground.

Aim On

There is a final bonus that I must share with you concerning dreaming with God. If you dare to dream with God, He will continually add details to what He has given you to be sure you are never done. God's dream will keep expanding like a mighty oak tree so it may bring Him more glory and help more people.

Once you begin to live the purpose God has for your life, He will see to it that your dream never ends. Nothing is more fulfilling or can compare with living out your purpose—the perfect will of God. Absolutely nothing!

13

THE EXHORTATION

I realize that some of you may have been seeking the Lord for many months or even years concerning your purpose in life. Perhaps you have even applied the principles we have covered. You have done all the seeking, praying, and talking with God you feel you can do, yet you still have not heard the first word about what He wants you to do with your life. You are discouraged and understandably so.

Don't lose heart all together. I have good news for you. The Lord does have something for you to do, and it is not something you have to wait ten years to put into practice. You can do it today! It is so simple that you may have already thought of it yourself yet sluffed it off as just another groping shot in the dark. But this is no desperation ploy. It is God's will.

Here it is: If you haven't as yet found your purpose in life, then find someone who has, and do anything and everything you can to help them get it done. That's right! Give yourself to *another's* vision instead of just sitting on your hands waiting for "lightning" to flash.

Hang In

God knows you are seeking Him, and He will reveal to you His perfect plan for your life. Don't even question that. But one thing is sure. He doesn't want you just to "hang around" until He does tell you your purpose. The Lord wants you to hang in and work together with the other members of His Body! Put your hand to the plow of another man's field until yours is secured for you.

As we saw in the chapter on the ministry of helps, this is a principle of sowing and reaping that you need to tap into *now* for use later. Also, you may not be called to any other purpose than the helps ministry. This isn't bad—it's great!

I'll even tell you where you should start your sowing—in your home church. Go talk to your pastor, elders, deacons, or whomever necessary, and let them know that you are available for service. Find a need that your gifts and talents can fill, and put the zeal of God to work for them through you. No church has too many volunteers. What other vision could be as rewarding as that of a local church reaching out to its surrounding community and possibly the world with the most important message in the universe? Get involved, and stay available.

When the Lord instructed me to pour the majority of my time into the vision of my pastor, a tremendous phenomenon occurred. Suddenly I began to receive more plans for my vision. It seemed that the more I worked for the church, regardless of what I was doing (be it menial labor or teaching the Bible), the more I heard from the Lord. It was the principle of sowing and reaping in action. It was working for me because I was working it. It will work for *you*, too.

Will your plan come to you immediately after you begin to give of your time and effort to your local body? I honestly don't know. I do know, however, that you will not only be opening yourself up to the return on what you have sown, but you will also be enjoying the satisfaction of seeing a vision come to pass before your very eyes.

Such on-the-job training can be invaluable when it comes to walking out *your* plan. You will be able to learn from the mistakes and successes of the church vision you work with and affect the lives of many in your community as well. Also, there is a good possibility that the very people you assist your church in ministering to will be the ones to help you with your purpose. No matter how you slice it, you come out on the good side of the deal.

So don't get discouraged if you have not yet received your purpose from the Lord. Be encouraged instead—encouraged by the possibility of learning from others as you prepare for your own vision.

Even if you never get a "full-blown" vision, such as we have discussed in this book, you will discover that being a part of another's vision is just as rewarding. How do I know that? Because you can never give away without receiving a return that is multiplied beyond what you invested. It's God's will. It's God's Word. It's God's way. Be excited! You can't lose! Hang in!

Hang On

Now for those of you who *have* a vision from the Lord for your life or have received it since beginning this book, I have exciting words for you, too. If you have been struggling with the walking out of your vision and feel that you may never see the fulfillment of it, Habakkuk 2:3 is a rock on which you can stand. The Lord promises here that the vision has an appointed time and that it will race toward the finish line. It will come to pass. It will be done. It will see fruition. Just hang on!

Sure it can be frustrating wanting to see the plan unfold a bit faster or the finish tape get a bit closer. But don't let the dark cloud of discouragement hang over you like a guillotine blade. Keep going. Stay excited. Take a look at how far you have already come. Get out your vision sheet, and daydream about it some more. It is on the way. The vision *will* happen.

In Hebrews 10:35-36, the Lord shares some powerful and encouraging insights with us:

> Therefore, do not throw away your con-
> fidence, which has a great reward. For
> you have need of endurance, so that
> when you have done the will of God,
> you may receive what was promised.

Did you get that? He told you not to throw away
your confidence. What confidence? Your confidence in God and your confidence in yourself.
That's right—yourself. You see, if you throw away
your confidence in *you*, then you have nothing
to work with. *God has confidence in you.* He
trusts you enough to give you a vision that will
steer your life down its appointed course. He trusts
you enough to give you a vision that will enlist
the lives of others who love Him. If He has such
confidence in you, then you can also.

Don't throw away your confidence in *God,*
either. He has yet to come up against an obstacle
in the life of one of His children that He could not
handle. You will not be the first! Jesus said, "With
God all things are possible." Between you and
God, your vision has everything needed to be a
divine success.

Verse thirty-six contains the real issue you must
deal with: endurance—patience—hanging on. It
is a problem for most of us, especially those with
a definite purpose to achieve. We want to please
our heavenly Father so much that we are quite
willing to run leagues ahead of Him to accomplish
our appointed task. Such hasty behavior is not

indicative of a life of confidence. The confiden
person is the one content to wait for God'
timing. After all, it is His will we wish to accom
plish. The reward spoken of is ours only after
patient performance of God's will.

Patience is ours. We don't even need to ask fo
it. Galatians 5:22 says it is part of the fruit of th
Spirit of God, and the Holy Spirit is in you as
believer in the Lord Jesus Christ. Therefore
asking for patience is unnecessary because it i
already within you.

What we need to do is *develop* that patience
Such development is only possible through tota
submission to the Lord's timing. At least acquir
ing it in the way He intends is only possible b
submitting. The zealot casts aside his patience an
rushes out to perform his vision ahead of God'
seemingly tortoise pace. But he will eventually en
up waiting for the Lord anyway as he gathers u
the pieces of his vision, which lie shattered by hi
haste. There are no shortcuts.

So don't let discouragement overtake you as yo
work through the steps of finding and living ou
your life's plan. Each step not only brings yo
closer to the fulfillment but builds within you th
fruit of patience as well. That patience wil
manifest itself in the joyous reward of you
Father's pleasure as you complete His will for you
life and help those you touch. Hang on to tha
promise in Habakkuk 2:3, and you will see th
vision hasten to completion.

Proverbs 4:20 explains that the Word of God is life to those who find it. Hebrews 4:12 states that His Word is filled with power. When the forces of discouragement close in, take God's Word and push them back to the pit where they belong. The Bible is our sword, and we must be skillful in wielding it for whatever we need. Here are a few verses I use to encourage myself when things seem to be closing in on me or on my vision:

> And Jesus said to him, " 'If you can!' All things are possible to him who believes"—Mark 9:23.

> And my God shall supply all your needs according to His riches in glory in Christ Jesus—Philippians 4:19.

> But thanks be to God, who always leads us in His triumph in Christ, and manifests through us the sweet aroma of the knowledge of Him in every place—2 Corinthians 2:14.

> But thanks be to God, who gives us the victory through our Lord Jesus Christ—1 Corinthians 15:57.

> But in all these things we overwhelmingly conquer through Him who loved us—Romans 8:37.

You are from God, little children, and have overcome them; because greater is He who is in you than he who is in the world—1 John 4:4.

For whatever is born of God overcomes the world; and this is the victory that has overcome the world—our faith—1 John 5:4.

With a vision in your heart, or having one on the way, you are walking in the realm of the highest form of living. To know that the plan laid before you is the perfect will of the Almighty God who created you and everything else—and to know that He is going to help you and send others to assist you in its completion—is the ultimate experience. It brings peace, joy, and life. Nothing compares to walking with God! Go for it with all you've got, and never give up. *You can do it!*

APPENDIX

SonDance: A Testimony

I have included this interview with my good friends, Joanne Cecere and Yvonne Peters, also known as the powerful dance ministry, Son-Dance, to illustrate the value of this work's teachings. When I met these two beautiful young ladies, I did not realize the magnitude of their anointing or the vastness of God's vision for them. I merely shared with them the principles contained within the pages of this book. Their progress from that first meeting has been somewhat meteoric, as you will read here.

BG: Why did you come to talk to me that first time?

SonDance: We came at that point because we were frustrated in our ministry. We wanted to do everything. We wanted to be evangelical, and we wanted to minister to the Body of Christ.

We wanted to accomplish the five-fold ministry, but didn't really know how to go about doing it. From time to time people would call us to minister at conferences or do local events, but not often. We were only dancing a couple of times a year back then. If we came up with a special piece, we could do it at our local church on a Sunday, but we weren't ministering on a regular basis.

Our dancing had a purpose to it, and we knew we were dancing under the anointing; but we didn't know where to move from there.

BG: What happened after you left my office that day?

SonDance: We left your office realizing we needed to state the purpose of our ministry. It caused us to refocus our thinking. We knew we had to think about what we were truly trying to accomplish and how to refine it. We wanted to minister to the Body of Christ *all* He was calling us to do. So, we decided to organize our priorities and focus on what God was anointing. Many of the things we had a heart to do weren't part of our call.

BG: How did you go about organizing and focusing?

SonDance: You spoke that day about planning. But when we came to you that morning, we were not able to plan eighteen *days* ahead. We didn't know what to plan, let alone how to plan. Now, just two years later in our ministry, we are preparing to plan an eighteen *month* calendar!

BG: We talked that day about planning practice sessions and prayer times.

Sondance: That's right. And that changed our entire course. It gave us a plan to start walking in. We didn't know how to set goals. In our immaturity, we just expected divine illumination. But, after receiving your counsel, the Lord told us, "Now you have to begin to use what I have given you and pick up the responsibility for what I have ahead of you." We had projects strewn from one end of the spectrum to the other, but we were too encumbered by work. By refocusing and setting some goals and priorities, we knew how to accomplish much more than we had in the past.

BG: What did you do specifically in your planning sessions?

SonDance: We practiced backward planning, and then we knew which direction to go in. We also learned not to set ten million goals but instead to concentrate on two and see if we could accomplish those.

BG: How did this help your ministry?

SonDance: One of the things you talked to us about was enlisting partners. You told us about intercessors—people who would pray for our ministry. Prior to that time, we had told people, "We are ministering one week out of the year. Please pray for us as we go." That was the extent of our prayer needs. Then God began to deal in *our* prayer lives about an organized daily prayer time. We focused that time on our goals.

As we began to pray more specifically, God laid an intercessory foundation in us. He then told us that He would send intercessors to help us pray for our goals. We began to look for them. Out of nowhere, people began to come up and say, "God has laid you on my heart." We began to send out an intercessors' letter, giving people a monthly prayer list of needs and goals. As we laid this foundation of setting practical goals and praying for them, the ministry changed drastically for the better.

Another major benefit was that we finally focused on what our true ministry was. We had experienced some frustration because we thought that our ministry had to be to the church, to the lost, *and* to support missions. We always tried to reach those goals but were never successful. Finally, we realized that our ministry is to the Church. It leads people to the throne. We know that now. But at that point, one of the mindsets of the church (and it was ours too) was, "So you went out to minister. How many souls were saved? How many baptisms in the Holy Spirit?" That was the measure of success in a ministry, and we were trying to force that on what the Lord had given us.

BG: That's not what He has called you to do? That was not His purpose for you?

SonDance: Correct. We didn't have the tools for it. The dance pieces we had were designed to minister to believers in the Church.

BG: So you had to be careful not to let the dictates of others, even believers, direct your vision. You had to seek the Lord continually for definite direction.

SonDance: Right. We had the vision, but we placed the wrong criteria on that vision. That changed as we matured and learned how to seek the Lord. I think prayer is the key. As you pray, seek, learn to wait, accept counsel, walk under submission, and get into a strong body of believers with a pastor who leads you, you begin to walk in the ways of God, and He unfolds the right vision to you.

BG: Why do you think goal setting and help from others in prayer was so effective?

SonDance: I think it was the seed principle you mentioned to us. The seed God gave you, you gave us. That impartation became a new vision in us. What you gave us caused us to focus our vision. Then our vision was able to multiply. Now God will do even more through those who have been seeded by us. When we took the seed of the vision that God placed in us, wrote it down, and shared it with others, that seed was put in them—along with the seed that God could give them their own visions.

BG: That's great! You say you have accomplished many things in just two years. Give me some details.

SonDance: First of all, God began to teach us to move people to worship through our dance.

Many believers expressed an interest in dance, so we began to hold workshops in various churches. Those workshops developed into dance troups which are now multiplying themselves!

BG: That's the exciting thing about a vision. Even though God gives you plans, He will always go beyond them to let you know that He is the One at work and not just you. What else have you done?

SonDance: The Lord also started giving us visions of routines in which we saw more dancers than just the two of us. Soon after that, He gave us opportunities to choreograph for groups of people and to be a part of worship teams at major conferences.

BG: What conferences have you done?

SonDance: We have performed at several of the *Christian Believers United* conferences. Now we are hooked up with the *Worship Symposium* ministry. Joanne choreographed "We Are Called" with David Wells. Also, God gave us an idea for a workshop, and we were invited to share it with the dancers who assembled at the *Feast of Tabernacles* conference in Jerusalem, Israel. We were involved with regional workshops through the *International Worship Symposium*. We have done some work for churches throughout the southeastern states, working with hundreds of dancers. We choreographed both "The Gospel According to Scrooge" and an Easter play at The Carpenter's Home Church in Lakeland, Florida.

(That church, by the way, has over 5,000 members, and over 50,000 people came to see "Scrooge" that year!) We also directed the *Festival of Praise* in Tampa, Florida. That was the largest dance group we had ever worked with.

BG: How many people were in that one?

SonDance: Forty-three dancers plus children.

BG: That's quite an impressive list of accomplishments in just two years. Tell me the most positive aspects about finding your purpose, walking it out, and applying all these different principles.

SonDance: One of the best was that we were able to go full-time in the dance ministry, which was, of course, the dream in our hearts from the beginning. It was the discipline and organization we put into practice that enabled us to be a full-time ministry.

One of the things you said that first meeting was, "Can you believe for a salary from the ministry?" At that point, *we* were supporting the ministry. *We* were giving the money every week. Your words echoed in our minds, and we talked about it later that week. Can we believe? We could! So we began to plan for it. Now the ministry does pay us a salary.

I believe one of the most important things you said was, "Get a vision for each goal." After that meeting with you, we listed everything that was happening in our ministry and wrote, "GET A VISION," over each item. That caused us to pray

and open ourselves to receive the vision for them
We had to have a different mindset. Th
mindset—to receive a vision on each item—ha
changed everything.

BG: Explain what "vision" means.

SonDance: Vision is begun by concentrating o
one area at a time, praying and meditating abou
that, and receiving from God as much as He ca
possibly reveal to you about that one particula
area. In the past two years, many parts of ou
vision have found completion. Now God is oper
ing new areas of our purpose to us.

Some things we had a vision for did not com
to pass. That doesn't mean those specific parts o
the vision have died, they have just not reache
their appointed time. However, if we did not *loo*
for them, *think* about them, and *pray* about the
in the first place, we probably would hav
dismissed those aspects of our purpose con
pletely. It is not that we see things crystal clea
immediately. The Lord gives us things to pra
about, and that starts the vision process.

BG: What you are saying is that God didn
reveal every step of the vision immediately, b
as you went, the next step was being revealed

SonDance: Right. Also, we have learned to loo
at it from God's perspective and not our own. It
like looking down and seeing the whole pictu
rather than just an isolated point. Also, I thir
vision is different from *goal*. I think we had mixe
them up and were trying to reach our visio

in terms of it being a goal. It was much too vast to accomplish until we broke it down into several separate goals.

BG: So what you are really saying is that you must have a vision before you can have a goal.

SonDance: That's right. If you don't have the vision first, you can't have a goal. A goal isn't vision. I think God set before us visions. You showed us how to set goals for those visions. Some things we could work on immediately, so we started there. Some were still in the vision stage, and the only goal we had was to pray about them. At first we didn't know about long-term and short-term goals. We thought everything was immediate.

BG: What are the problems involved in finding and living out your purpose in such an organized manner?

SonDance: Some of my (Yvonne) frustrations are that I am not as organized as I would like to be. I would really like to refine things.

BG: Do you mean that this kind or organization shows you how unorganized you are?

SonDance: Yes. But, also, I (Joanne) am an organizer by nature. I start organizing big things and organize down, down, down. Suddenly, I have organized so much, I have no time for the meat or the creativity—the actual workings of it. That is a flaw I know I battle against.

We are learning to combat frustration by allocating and are in the process of trying to develop a helps ministry. Two people can't run this ministry anymore—it is much bigger than two. We are so encompassed in the network of organization that we hardly ever have time to create. We are starting to get stale.

BG: You mean you can get so caught up in the business administration end of your vision that you end up planning all the time and leave no time for creativity?

SonDance: That's right. Management becomes the goal. You can't let that run you. It is not a *business* we are running but a *ministry*. The strength of our ministry was that we prayed together, danced together, and worshipped together. Those are three things we find very hard to do anymore for lack of time.

BG: Is the problem that you are getting so caught up in the system that it isn't allowing you to function in the very thing it was created to help you do?

SonDance: Exactly. You serve the system instead of the system serving you. So, as we said, we are now forced to allocate some of our work so we can have at least one day off to be creative. No paperwork is to be done on that day, and we leave it open to spend with the Lord and each other and to create. It used to be the opposite. We used to dance all the time and schedule one work day. Now we work all the time and schedule one dance day!

BG: Would you say that time management is an important aspect of your vision?

SonDance: Absolutely! And still there is frustration with scheduling. We have to say "No" to some requests for our ministry. We used to accept anyone who asked us to come. Now we have to go to our calendar and ask, "Can we?" Time management has definitely been good for us—both in daily and long-range areas.

BG: So, two years ago you had a vision. You knew that God was calling you to a dance ministry, but you didn't know exactly how to go about it. You had come to the place that you were doing everything you knew how to do but were not progressing.

SonDance: We had a call. I'm not sure we had a vision. When we came to you, we just knew that what we were doing was of God. Up until then, we had been dancing and ministering for five years—not a lot, but we believe it was a valid ministry. In the last two years, however, it has exploded.

BG: So where are you now in your purpose?

SonDance: We still have some goals planned for this year that havn't been accomplished, and since there is one more month to go, we are scrambling to get them done. That is the nice thing about knowing your purpose and having it planned out. If something doesn't get done today, it will still be there tomorrow. Those goals we don't accomplish will be first on the list next year.

BG: One last question. If God told you today to stop and do no more, what would you do?

SonDance: We would have to stop because every day our highest will is to be obedient to the Father. The vision cannot be our god. The ministry cannot be our god. Jesus must be our God. If He said today, "Stop", it wouldn't be the first time either of us have heard that. It is not an unfamiliar word. At one point we had to do that almost daily. You can't receive or assume any identity because of your vision. You are made to conform to the image of Jesus Christ on a daily basis.

It is easy to get so caught up in what you do that you make your vision become who you are. We can try to hold on to an unauthorized identity, but that is not right. We have to be willing to let it go. We want to do and be what God wants us to do and be.

BG: Do you think God requires everyone to do that? Do you think Christians must come to the point where they say, "The vision isn't going to be my God."?

SonDance: Yes. We don't think He can really move like He wants to until the death of that vision comes. You can begin to think *for* God instead of listening *to* God. There is a real danger there. Also, whatever your conception of success is, you may begin to feed that to your vision. It is very dangerous. Our will must be to do the will of our Father. If that means walking away from our vision, then that is what we will do. I believe that's what everyone must be able to do.

Joanne and Yvonne are two Christian believers like you and me. But their impact on the Church exploded with divine force almost "overnight" because they chose to find their purpose in life and live it out. I pray that their candid reflections on how they applied these principles will inspire you to do the same with your God-ordained purpose.

"And whatever you do in word and deed, do all in the name of the Lord Jesus, giving thanks through Him to God the Father" (Colossians 3:17).

For information in regard to scheduling Mr. Greenman's *How To Find Your Purpose In Life* seminar for your church, or to obtain seminar tapes and workbooks, please call (813) 985-7846 or write:

"Purpose"
P.O. Box 16889
Temple Terrace, FL 33687